Keep Up the Good Faith

A Muslim Woman's Perspective on Career, Marriage and Life

AIYEN SEGOVIA

Published by:

Unit No. E-10-5, Jalan SS 15/4G, Subang Square,
47500 Subang Jaya, Selangor, Malaysia
+603-7772-3156 (office) / +6017-399-7411 (mobile)
info@tertib.press
www.tertib.press
@tertibpress (Facebook & Instagram)

Author	:	Aiyen Segovia
Editor	:	Norashikin Azizan
Cover designer	:	Abdul Adzim Md Daim
Typesetter	:	Abdul Adzim Md Daim

KEEP UP THE GOOD FAITH

First Edition: June 2022

Perpustakaan Negara Malaysia   Cataloguing-in-Publication Data

Aiyen Segovia
Keep Up The Good Faith / Aiyen Segovia.
ISBN 978-967-2844-18-1
1. Aiyen Segovia--Anecdotes.
2. Muslim women--Anecdotes.
3. Muslim women--Conduct of life--Anecdotes.
4. Women in the professions--Anecdotes.
5. Married women--Anecdotes.
I. Title.
808.882

CONTENTS

INTRODUCTION	1
DEDICATION	3
CHAPTER 1: REMINDERS TO SELF	4
1: The People of *Shahadah*	5
2: Diverse Spiritual Personality	7
3: The 'Envious' Friend	9
4: Knowledge and Fear of Allah	11
5: The Miracles of the Qur'an	13
6: Ten Years Challenge	15
7: The Brightest Star	18
8: The Overlooked Blessings	20
9: Emptiness and Broken Heart	22
10: Blessing to the *Ummah*	25
11: Striving to be Useful	27
12: How to be You?	28
13: Faith Goals	30
14: Maintaining Strong *Iman*	32
15: The Power of One Minute	34

16: A *Ṣadaqah* Millionaire!	37
17: *Dhikr Sayyidul Istighfar*	*40*
18: Nevertheless, They Persisted	43
19: Change of Hearts	45
20: Real Manhood	47
21: Be Mindful of Allah	49

CHAPTER 2: THE JOURNEY OF SEEKING HALAL *RIZQ* — 50

22: The Best Charity	51
23: *Deen* Over Money	53
24: On-Call Story	55
25: His Story of Miracle	57
26: Blessings In Disguise	59
27: *Rizq* After *Nikaḥ*	62
28: Work Hard, Pray Harder	64
29: The Blessed Income	67
30: The Foundation of *Rizq*	70
31: Moderation In Spending and Giving	72

CHAPTER 3: THE BEAUTY OF MARRIAGE — 75

32: Marry for *Deen*	76
33: *Nikaḥ* is a Blessing	78
34: The Bridal Speech—Her Faith, His Destiny	81
35: Self-Betterment Through Marriage	85
36: Partner to Heaven	87
37: Rejoice Love Every Day	89
38: Be the Water In a Fire	91

39: The Unspoken Sacrifices   93

40: Romanticism   95

41: Keep It Halal   97

42: The Love Letter   99

43: My Man   103

44: A Child to His Wife   105

45: A Grateful Wife   106

46: An Open Letter to the Future Married Couples   108

CHAPTER 4: THE ROAD TO PARENTHOOD   110

47: A Gift from Heaven   111

48: A Woman's Jihad   114

49: The Islamic Responsibility of a Mother   117

50: The Glory of Motherhood   120

51: The Power of a Mother's Prayers   122

52: My Wonderful VBAC Experience   124

53: Siddique and Farooque   126

54: Knowing Allah Through Motherhood   128

55: Motherhood Getaway   130

56: The 'Underrated' Dads   133

57: To Love with Discipline   135

CHAPTER 5: LESSONS LEARNED IN LIFE   138

58: Listen to Your Self-Talk   139

59: Now or Never   141

60: Make a Flower Bloom   144

61: The Abused Kindness   146

62: The *Barakah* of Time — 149

63: Retention is by Repetition — 153

64: Great Things Take Time — 155

65: Garden of Paradise — 157

66: A Teacher for Life — 160

67: A Journey of Teaching Children — 163

68: The Gift That Keeps Giving — 167

69: Back In 2012 — 170

70: Behind the Bars — 172

71: Taiwan Takeaways — 174

72: Venice—Little Wish Granted — 177

73: Covid-19: Tomorrow is Not Promised — 179

74: Covid-19: Absence of Fear — 181

75: Covid-19: Choose to Spread Positivity — 184

INTRODUCTION

*In the name of Allah, the Most Gracious,
the Most Merciful.*

Keep Up the Good Faith: A Muslim Woman's Perspective on Career, Marriage and Life, is an open diary that initially was written down as a personal journal for the author to always be mindful and thankful. It is about life struggles and lessons based on inspiring true stories that occurred as the author grew up and those whom she met along the way. The stories in this book are worth years of experiences—the struggles from being a student to a worker to a mother; life lessons from singlehood to parenthood; challenges as a friend, a teacher, a traveller, and many more.

The articles compiled in this book are composed of random personal insights as well as real-life experiences with the Qur'an, authentic *aḥadith*, sayings of the scholars or relevant *du'a'* (supplications) attached. Each piece is short and perfect for a quick read, but it comes with precise points and a meaningful vision.

As this book was finally published, it serves the purpose that the readers can somehow connect it with real current life struggles and find ways to keep up their good faith in Allah despite the never-ending battles.

DEDICATION

To the One, who bestowed upon me too many blessings to count.

To my parents, who raised me well.

To my mother-in-law, for being the first to believe in my writing skill.

To my husband, the one who pushed me to publish a book.

To my siblings, for the never-ending support.

To my friends, who compliment and criticise my piece of art.

May Allah accept this book as a deed and reward you all as much as He will reward me for this book. Ameen.

CHAPTER 1: REMINDERS TO SELF

"And remind, for indeed, the reminder benefits the believers."

[adh-Dhariyat, 51:55]

1: The People of *Shahadah*

"Why haven't you graduated? It has been years."

"Why aren't you hired yet? It has been years."

"Why aren't you promoted yet? It has been years."

"Why aren't you married yet? It has been years."

"Why aren't you pregnant yet? It has been years"

Some graduated early, some graduated late, while others do not graduate at all. But what is early? What is late? Compared to whom? We are constantly worrying about the next part of our lives without realising that we are right in the middle of what we used to look forward to.

Bear in mind, we are the people of *shahadah* (testimony to Islam) and we believe in destiny. If you have tried your best and have done what was humanly possible to achieve your goals, then have faith. Most people mistake it as false hope. But deep down you know, the soul understands that what Allah gives is a gift, what Allah delays is also a gift.

Just like a knife that serves as a kitchen tool for a mother, it is also dangerously sharp for a five-year-old daughter. Hence, a knife is a blessing to the mother but a curse to the daughter. You see, a certain thing will be a blessing if it is given at the right time but turns out to be a curse if it comes too soon.

Try to apply this principle in everything. For we are believers, and we believe in *al-Qadr* (predestination). A single leaf does not fall without His permission, do you think He has not thought about your future?

"And with Him are the keys of the unseen; none knows them except Him. And He knows what is on the land and in the sea. Not a leaf falls but that He knows it. And no grain is there within the darknesses of the earth and no moist or dry [thing] but that it is [written] in a clear record."

[al-An'am, 6:59]

So, please be gentle with yourself in everything, you are doing the best you can. Being both soft and strong, is a combination very few have mastered.

2: Diverse Spiritual Personality

Some of us find fasting is easy, but difficult to recite the Qur'an. Some of us have no time for *sunnah* (supplementary) prayers but have extra money for charity. Some of us are very eager in pursuing Islamic knowledge but are quite hard to wake up for *tahajjud* (night prayer).

Every believer wishes to be the best they can be and embrace every aspect of righteous deeds, but it depends on our individual nature that we might naturally find certain deeds are easier to be done, while still struggling with other deeds, for example fasting versus *tahajjud*.

Even Imam Malik of Madinah spends his time in circles of knowledge rather than the other aspects of faith, such as working directly in his Muslim society. He responded by explaining the idea of a spiritual personality, similar to the way we would understand our human personality.

> "Say, 'Each works according to his manner, but your Lord is most knowing of who is best guided in way'."
>
> [al-Isra', 17:84]

So, as long as we are upon righteousness and goodness, do not feel discouraged to think that what we are focusing on now has lesser value compared to what other people are doing. We are all different and should not impose our lifestyles on each other.

May Allah grant our hearts to love the deeds we find difficult to make a habit of doing and grant more love on the deeds that we already naturally love doing. *Ameen*.

3: The 'Envious' Friend

In a world full of insecure people being bitter to other people's happiness, let us be among those who admire and are inspired by other people's achievements, success, and happy life. Verily, a soul of envy only comes from a heart that is not contented with how Allah distributed His blessings.

To be contented with something does not mean that you must be personally happy about it. We can be content, in a moment of happiness or sadness, or success and failure. This is because to be truly contented is actually to be fully thankful for whatever Allah has ordained for us be it good or bad. Contentment is thus another level of submission to Allah.

When we train our souls to embrace the true definition of contentment, we will not be troubled by what others have. Even when the eyes fall for what others have of worldly blessings, a contented heart will direct its spirit to look not on their gifts but rather the Giver of Gifts, the Most Generous, the Provider of *rizq* (provision). The people who say "*Alḥamdulillah*" in every situation will still see the beauty of scenery even when the weather is gloomy; even when the trees are dead.

However, let us be jealous of two types of people—those whom Allah has given wealth and they spend it righteously, and those whom Allah has given the wisdom of knowledge and they teach it to others.

The Prophet (peace be upon him) said,

"Do not wish to be like anyone except in two cases. (The first is) A person, whom Allah has given wealth and he spends it righteously; (the second is) the one whom Allah has given wisdom (the Holy Qur'an) and he acts according to it and teaches it to others."

[Ṣaḥih al-Bukhari]

We need to pray to be blessed with such gifts. If you already have a job, try to allocate some amount for charity every month even just RM5. If you know how to recite Qur'an, offer to voluntarily teach children *alif ba ta* in your neighbourhood. We can make a change in our little way.

In the event of seeing other people's success, draw your motivation from them instead of creating unnecessary jealousy. Remember, what you see in other people is a reflection of yourself. A person of goodness will always see goodness in others.

The Prophet Muhammad (peace be upon him) said,

"Beware of jealousy. For verily it destroys good deeds the way fire destroys wood."

[Sunan Abi Dawud]

4: Knowledge and Fear of Allah

Somewhere in a city, there is a man who loves his wife so much but his wife does not love him anymore. The wife has been seeking *'ilm (knowledge)* for so long while the husband has to work hard searching *rizq (provision)* to meet his family's basic needs. The wife is fluent in Arabic, but the husband knows only his mother tongue. The wife has memorised a lot of Qur'anic verses, but the husband does not have the luxury of time to do so.

It is sad to see how her knowledge does not increase her love towards her husband rather it deceives her into thinking she should deserve someone better than him. She has been deluded by her intelligence so much so that her husband has no value at all in her eyes.

She memorised the hadith that says "Look at how you are with him, for he is your paradise and your hell." [Musnad Aḥmad] and "If only humans can prostrate to each other, then surely a wife should prostrate to her husband because of the greatness of rights he has over her." [Sunan Abi Dawud], yet how come she does not take heed from these?

"Verily, knowledge is not knowing many narrations but knowledge is the fear of Allah."

[Rawdat al-'Uqala]

It could be that she has more knowledge than her husband, but her husband has more fear of Allah. It could be that she has more advantages than her husband, but her husband is more beloved to Allah because of his *tawadu'* (humility).

Some sisters are making *sunnah* fasting without their husband's permission, refuse their husband's call to bed as they want to stand for *tahajjud*, isolate themselves in seeking knowledge thus neglecting their husband's rights. Many of us failed to realise that our husband is actually our *FIELD OF REWARDS*.

Ibn Ḥibban narrated that Abu Hurayrah said:

The Prophet (peace be upon him) said: "If a woman prays her five (daily prayers), fasts her month (Ramadan), guards her chastity and obeys her husband, it will be said to her: 'Enter Paradise from whichever of the gates of Paradise you wish.'"

[Ṣaḥih ibn Ḥibban]

May Allah grant us beneficial knowledge!

5: The Miracles of the Qur'an

From the *barakah* (blessings) of the Qur'an is that Allah blesses the mind of the one who reads it and memorises it. Without we realise it or not, reciting the Qur'an somehow helps to sharpen our minds.

The recitation of the Qur'an demands a lot of processes to be done at once. To accomplish perfection during our Qur'an recitation, we have to distinguish the letters accurately, know the characteristics of each letter correctly, carry out their precise *makhraj* (points of articulation of letters), connect it with the next letter together with *fatḥah* (´) or *kasrah* (.) or *ḍammah* (´) as well as figure out their *tajwid* (Qur'an recitation rules) for *izhar* (to make clear), *idgham* (to merge), *mad* (lengthening), and many more—all at once!

Meanwhile, while our eyes are reading, our mouths are reciting them simultaneously requiring the brain to decide quickly for us to have a smooth recitation. What makes the Qur'an even more unique is that it must be read from right to left.

Also, without realising it or not, we tend to recite the Qur'an melodiously which naturally renders our soul a relaxing therapy. Perhaps that is why we do not feel tired mentally though our brain is working hard that time.

'Abdul Malik ibn 'Umair is narrated to have said,

"It used to be said that the ones whose minds stayed [sharp and clear] longest were the reciters of the Qur'an."

Al-Qurṭubi said,

"Whoever reads the Qur'an enjoys his mind even if he reaches one hundred [years]."

Indeed, the recitation of the Qur'an is in itself a miracle. *Allahuakbar.*

6: Ten Years Challenge

The knowledge of proper *tajwid* and the ability to recite the Qur'an smoothly are fruits of thousands of efforts and practices. And even so, we will never stop learning the Qur'an for the rest of our lives as no matter how good we are, we are still capable of making random mistakes and stumbling upon reciting.

Therefore, do not make your inability to recite Arabic letters a source of disconnection with the messages of Allah. If you do not know how to recite them, then inspire yourself to at least read the translation.

Day by day we keep studying hard to improve our grades, working hard to earn more income, struggling hard to be promoted. We are willing to sacrifice so much for *dunya* (worldly) achievements but why when it comes to the *deen* (religion), our Qur'an understanding keeps stagnant at the same level for ten years and never seems to increase? For the non-Arabs like us, how many of us have read the all the thirty *juz* (chapter) translation of the Qur'an?

If only ten years ago we were determined to recite one verse one day with translation, by today we already internalised half of the Qur'an! But it is never too late to start now, let us understand the words of Allah even just a verse a day. To act upon the Qur'an, we need to understand it not just merely memorise it.

Ibn al-Qayyim said:

"If the people knew the sweetness, and benefits in pondering over the Qur'an when reading it, they would have kept themselves busy with nothing else but reading the Qur'an. For reading and pondering over one verse is better than a *khatma* (completion of the whole Qur'an) without contemplation nor understanding. It is also more beneficial to the heart, attains *iman* (faith) and makes one taste the sweetness of the Qur'an."

[Miftaḥ Dar al-Saʿadah]

Verily, the understanding and contemplation upon the Qur'anic verses bring heavier impact to the soul than just plain recitation. The Qur'an was not sent down only for those who "have a beautiful voice" or "have melodious recitation" or "understand Arabic", it is for all. Guidance for you and me, even the non-Muslims.

So have your favourite pocket Qur'an translation and who knows, by the end of the year, we have read the Qur'an by heart and may Allah ease our ways to memorise and act upon it. *In shaa Allah.*

"Increase your recitation of the Qur'an and do not leave it; for what you seek will be facilitated to you by the amount you read."

[Dhayl Ṭabaqat al-Ḥanabilah]

7: The Brightest Star

May we be strengthened with the understanding that being blessed does not mean that we always are spared from all the disappointments or difficulties of life. Blessed are those who see the signs and mercy of Allah even in failures.

If you are afflicted with harm despite regularly reciting *adhkar (remembrance of Allah)*, or when your *du'a'* made in *tahajjud* were not granted, remember that all of these were from the decree of Allah as a test to our faith.

'Ikrimah narrated from Ibn 'Abbas that he said:

"The angels will protect us from in front and from behind, but when the decree of Allah comes, they step back."

[Tafsir ibn Kathir]

In trusting Allah, sometimes what is best for us might be what is most painful to us. So, to be able to say, "*Alhamdulillah 'ala kulli ḥal*" despite the disappointment is the greatest test of faith and demonstrates strong *tawakkul* (reliance on Allah).

It was narrated that Abu Hurayrah said:

"The Messenger of Allah (peace be upon him) said:
'The strong believer is better and more beloved to

Allah than the weak believer, although both are good. Strive for that which will benefit you, seek the help of Allah, and do not feel helpless if anything befalls you, do not say, "if only I had done such and such" rather say *"Qaddara Allahu wa ma sha'a fa'ala "* (Allah has decreed and whatever he wills, he does)." For (saying) 'If' opens (the door) to the deeds of Satan."

[Sunan ibn Majah]

I pray that you and I will be among the people who can fully embrace the essence of *tawakkul*—the ones who continue to make *du'a'* despite the rejection, to keep loving despite the heartbreaks, to keep giving despite the nothingness—as we strongly rely on Allah for rewards.

The Prophet (peace be upon him) said,

"How excellent the affairs of the believer: his affair, all of it, is good for him; and this is not the case with anyone except the believer; if prosperity comes to him, he is thankful (to God), and if adversity falls on him, he perseveres patiently: so it is all good (for him)"

[Ṣaḥih Muslim]

La taḥzan. It is often in the darkest sky, that we see the brightest stars.

8: The Overlooked Blessings

If you can go to school every day, study hard, pay the tuition fee and take exams peacefully, then there already lie countless blessings to be thanked for. Out there is someone who is sick and cannot get out of bed, others who cannot pursue education because they have to work, some do not have money even just for a pencil, and many other obstacles.

> "And He gave you from all you asked of Him. And if you should count the favour of Allah, you could not enumerate them. Indeed, mankind is [generally] most unjust and ungrateful.
>
> [Ibrahim, 14:34]

We always think that only those who passed their exams are the blessed ones. But you see, being able to take exams regardless of the results, is composed of many uncountable blessings already.

Therefore, whenever you failed your exam and feel down, look for strength by reminding yourself that you are still beyond blessed. When you have to "try again next time" or "shift course", at least you have alternatives that some people cannot even dream about.

The Prophet Muhammad (peace be upon him) said,

"When one of you sees another who is superior to him in point of wealth and creation, let him look to him who is below him. That is more proper that you hold not in contempt the favour of God towards you"

[Ṣaḥiḥ al-Bukhari and Muslim]

Seek for the overlooked blessings, and say *Alḥamdulillah 'ala kulli ḥal.'*

9: Emptiness and Broken Heart

Have you ever wanted to cry but no tears came out, so you just stare blankly into space while feeling your heart breaks into pieces?

Being depressed out of heartbreak is brutally painful. Being heartbroken does not only occur when someone dies. When you failed your exam, your heart broke. When you lost your job, your heart broke. When you were left by someone you love, your heart broke. When you were diagnosed with a disease, your heart broke.

Similarly, there are moments in our lives when we suddenly feel empty too. We were not heartbroken. But somehow, we have that feeling of being blank, being numb or being sad without reason. This is well explained in a hadith:

"If the sins of a servant are numerous and he does not have good deeds to compensate, then Allah afflicts him with sadness as an expiation for him."

[Musnad Aḥmad]

We just have to understand, that depression is not quantitative. What sadness you have cannot be compared to the sadness someone else has. The intensity of what you feel about something is unique to you. And as humans, we do not deal well with emptiness. That is why we run from an attachment to another attachment, or worse, we run from destruction to another destruction. For some of us, a sin is an attempt to flee from emptiness yet it only causes us more sadness.

Imam Ibn al-Qayyim (Allah has mercy on him) said,

"Perhaps one sin will be the cause for long term sadness."

[al-Fawaid]

While for some of us, it is through the emptiness that we find faith. It is only by experiencing pain, that we realise faith is what helps us heal.

"No disaster strikes upon the earth or among yourselves except that it is in a register before We bring it into being—indeed that, for Allah, is easy. In order that you not despair over what has eluded you and not exult [in pride] over what He has given you. And Allah does not like everyone self-deluded and boastful."

[al-Ḥadid, 57:22-23]

In unexplained emotional breakdowns like these, let the

believers be reminded to return to Allah, recite the Qur'an, repeat *dhikrullah*, say *istighfar* (seeking forgiveness) non-stop. Turn the emptiness into a "possibility yet to be filled". Mend the broken heart to a faithful mind that surrenders to Allah.

It is only when you accept your nothingness that you are forced to fill your soul with abundance remembrance of Allah, because deep down, you know it is your only hope to let your heart regain its tranquillity again.

> "Those who have believed and whose hearts are assured by the remembrance of Allah. Unquestionably, by the remembrance of Allah's hearts are assured."
>
> [ar-Ra'd, 13:28]

10: Blessing to the *Ummah*

Sometimes, we created stress out of nothing simply because we aimed for perfection. We vow not to settle with any result less than that. I agree with what a friend said, that people like these did their best in everything they do, not because they wanted to be known for their excellence. Rather, it is by striving for perfection that they can maximise their potential and thus be beneficial as much as possible to others.

Just like Juwairiyah bint al-Harith who is known as the woman of blessing to her people, as hundreds of her people were freed from captivity due to her marriage to the Prophet Muhammad (peace be upon him). We too, in our way and the best possible manner, also should dream to be a blessing to our community or at least, to the people we love.

Prophet Muhammad (peace be upon him) said,

"The most beloved people to Allah are those who are most beneficial to the people."

[al-Mu'jam al-Awsat]

Therefore, as Muslims who claim to embody Islam, we should always strive to practise perfection in our daily life. We believe that a Muslim must strive hard to be an outstanding role model to the world by demonstrating a balanced pursuit of excellence in both worldly and religious matters, as it serves as *da'wah* (a call to embrace Islam) itself and ultimately improves the public perception of Islam.

So wherever you are now and whatever you do, especially in moments when you are feeling tired and wanting to give up, find the inspiration so you can force yourself to be your best again—as a student, as an employee, as a child, as a spouse, as a parent, as a friend and as a Muslim—to give justice to Islam's purity and be a source of blessing to this *ummah* (Muslim community).

11: Striving to be Useful

In this era of Instagram and TikTok where many strive to be famous, instead, strive to be useful. People who crave fame will always need validation, but people who strive to be useful will always be found.

Learn from the Prophets and be possessed by the desire to be useful for Allah on this Earth. Prophet Dawud (peace be upon him) was a blacksmith, Zakariyya (peace be upon him) a carpenter and Idris (peace be upon him) a tailor; yet they were the best of humankind. They benefitted people, not by some fame or financial status, but because they used their talents and all the bounties that they were given correctly.

Indeed, our value is in our abilities and contributions to society. Be useful and inspire to live a life that will be a testimony of success.

"So race to [all that is] good."

[al-Baqarah, 2:148]

One day, we will be just a memory to some people. Let us do our best to be a good one.

12: How to be You?

I think as humans we will always be amazed at the super-rich, super intelligent, super pretty and handsome, super talented and other extraordinary people.

But as Muslims, nothing beats the 'halal jealousy' we have towards the super-rich who spend their money on the path of Allah; the pretty women and handsome men who also memorised the Qur'an and can recite it beautifully with perfect *tajwid*; the intelligent people who utilise their skills for the benefits of this *ummah*; and all kinds of people who have been blessed by Allah with something phenomenal yet they use those blessings only to earn *Jannah* (paradise). Like *masha Allah*, how to be you?

In our Islamic vocabulary, they are the ones who are truly impressive and worthy to be jealous of. For how many unthankful hearts discover no fear in their Lord despite their heavenly blessings?

"They recognise the favour of Allah; then they deny
it. And most of them are disbelievers."

[an-Naḥl, 16:83]

May we always be grateful to Allah's favour upon us.

"My Lord, enable me to be grateful for Your favour which You have bestowed upon me and upon my parents and to work righteousness of which You will approve and make righteous for me my offspring. Indeed, I have repented to You, and indeed, I am of the Muslims."

[al-Aḥqaf, 46:15]

13: Faith Goals

Just like career goals, travel goals, friendship goals and many others, we also need to have faith goals because it is not like we are going to wake up one day and suddenly be an excellent Muslim right away. We need to set daily and life goals for ourselves. Nothing is just going to come to us easily.

We. Have. To. Try.

Minimum daily faith goals suggestion: Pray five times a day; read and understand the Qur'an at least one page; *ḍuḥa* (morning supplementary prayer); *witr* (supplementary prayer done between after Isha prayer and before Subuh prayer); recite morning and evening *adhkar.*

Lifetime faith goals suggestion:

1.   Aim to keep memorising the Qur'an as long as we live

2.   Keep attending beneficial classes as long as we live

3.   Donate at least once in a lifetime:

  •   A Qur'an to someone

  •   Fund to building of masjid/madrasah/*da'wah*

  •   A prayer mat or dress for someone

4.   Sponsor as long as we are able:

- A student who seeks knowledge in the path of Allah

- A widow and her orphans

- A meal to someone who is fasting

5. Teach at least one person:

- A beneficial *du'a'*

- Qur'an recitations

- One good deed

- A *sunnah* (Prophet's tradition)

With all the life goals, we will always feel busy. But it is not enough just to be busy, because the ants are also busy. The question is, what is your life busy about? We are all given the same amount of time in a day, yet why do we all succeed in very different lengths? Be productive and be the best version of yourself. Master your energy. Master your focus. Master your time.

اللَّهُمَّ أَعِنِّيْ عَلَى ذِكْرِكَ وَشُكْرِكَ وَحُسْنِ عِبَادَتِكَ

"Allahumma a'inni 'ala dhikrika wa shukrika wa husni 'ibadatika."

(O' Allah! Assist me in remembering You, in thanking You, and in worshipping You in the best of manners.)

[Musnad Aḥmad]

14: Maintaining Strong *Iman*

Ever felt like you're having an *iman* dip? That after being a very active, productive Muslim—praying on time, reading the Qur'an frequently, always looking forward to doing good deeds—you are becoming lazy and that your enthusiasm to perform the same way is fading?

Below are among the bits of advice extracted from Ustadh Dr Khalid Basalamah's lecture on how to be *istiqamah* (consistent) in keeping up with the good faith. May this benefit.

1. **Keep listening to Islamic lectures for a consistent spiritual boost**

   Watch beneficial YouTube videos, keep attending circles of knowledge, read good books or arrange a list of mp3 Islamic lectures on your phone to listen to every day. No matter how busy we are, never leave the path of seeking knowledge! This is always the key to *iman* boost.

2. **Practice what you have learned**

   'Ibadah (worship) must be forced sometimes. Force yourself to wake up for *tahajjud*. Force yourself to read the Qur'an. Sometimes out of the struggle of forcing ourselves in seeking the pleasure of Allah, only then

do we find sincerity, addiction, and sweetness of faith. *In shaa Allah.*

3. Follow only positive pages and friends

You are what you read and whom you surround yourself with. Do not follow negative accounts or those who do not add value to your life.

Another to-boost-*iman*-list:

- Recite the Qur'an with translation one page per day.

- Finish one good book every week.

- Look for potential receivers and make a *ṣadaqah* (charity) list every month.

Abdullah ibn Amr reported:

The Messenger of Allah, peace be upon him, said, "Verily, the faith of one of you will diminish just as a shirt becomes worn out, so ask Allah to renew faith in your hearts."

[al-Mustadrak]

15: The Power of One Minute

With just one minute, you can receive sustenance from unimagined and unexpected sources. How?

Recite "*astaghfirullāh*" 100 times.

[Sunan Abi Dawud]

With just one minute, more weight will be added to your *mizan* (scale) and you will also earn the pleasure of Allah. How?

Recite "*SubḥānAllāhi wa biḥamdihi subḥānAllāhil 'adhīm*".

[Ṣaḥih al-Bukhari]

With just one minute, you can have the treasure from the treasures of Paradise. How?

Say "*Lā hawla wa lā quwwata illā billāh*".

[Ṣaḥih at-Tirmidhi]

With just one minute, a palm tree will be planted for you in Paradise. How?

Say "*SubḥānAllāhil 'adhīmi wa biḥamdihi*".

[Ṣaḥih at-Tirmidhi]

With just one minute, you can build a palace in Paradise. How?

By reciting *Surah al-Ikhlas* ten times.

[Musnad Aḥmad]

With just one minute, Allah will exalt to your mention ten times, ten of your sins will be removed and you will be raised ten degrees. How?

By saying "*Allāhumma ṣalli wa sallim ʿala Nabiyyina Muḥammad*".

[Ṣaḥih Muslim]

Al-Ḥasan al-Baṣri said,

"All actions come to an end, except *dhikr* (remembrance of Allah). It has no break or end."

A believer lives upon *dhikr* dies upon it and is resurrected upon it.

Ibn al-Qayyim said,

"*Nur* (radiance) of *dhikr* remains with a person in his life and his grave. It will guide him on the *sirat* (hair-narrow bridge) in the Hereafter."

16: A Ṣadaqah Millionaire!

Everyone will be blown away when reading the biography of billionaire Sulaiman al-Rajhi. Saudi Arabia's rags-to-riches billionaire Sulaiman al-Rajhi is also a world-renowned philanthropist. He is the founder of al-Rajhi Bank, the largest Islamic bank in the world. As of 2011, his wealth was estimated by Forbes to be $7.7 billion, making him the 120th richest person in the world. His flagship SAAR Foundation is a leading charity organisation in the Kingdom of Saudi Arabia. The Al-Rajhi family is considered one of the Kingdom's wealthiest non-royals and among the world's leading philanthropists.

How very blessed are the wealthy religious people, they can grab all the rewards? They pray the way we pray; they fast the way we fast, but they can do more charity than we can. How can we ever achieve their rank? In *Surah al-Munafiqun* verse 10, Allah said that the people who have died wished to come back to life so they could perform charity. The scholars explained that they requested to do charity, instead of fasting or *ḥajj* (pilgrimage) or any other good deeds, was because they have seen how big the reward of charity is!

Fortunately, Prophet Muhammad (peace be upon him) taught us how to overtake them! No one will excel us except they do what we do!

All we have to do is to recite *SubhanAllah* thirty-three times, *Alhamdulillah* thirty-three times, *Allahuakbar* thirty-three times, every after *salah* (prayer) and if we follow it with *"Lā ilaha illĀllahu wahdahu lā sharīka lah, lahul mulku wa lahul hamdu wa huwa 'ala kulli shay 'in qadir"* complete a hundred, our sins will be forgiven even if they are as abundant as the foam of the sea!

Abu Hurayrah (May Allah be pleased with him) reported:

The poor Emigrants came to the Messenger of Allah (peace be upon him) and said: "The wealthy have gone with the highest ranks and lasting bliss." He asked: "How is that? They replied: "They offer *salah* (prayer) as we offer it; they observe fast as we do; (and as they are wealthy) they perform *hajj* and "umrah and go for jihad (war), and they spend in charity but we cannot, and they free the slaves but we are unable to do so." The Messenger of Allah (peace be upon him) said," "Shall I not tell you a thing, by doing which, you will catch up with those who are ahead of you and supersede those who will come after you; None will excel you unless he who does which you do." They said: "Yes, please do, O' Messenger of Allah." He (peace be upon him) said, "You should recite: tasbih (*SubhanAllah*), takbir (*Allahuakbar*), tahmid (*Alhamdulillah*) thirty-three times after each *salah*."

[Ṣahih al-Bukhari and Muslim]

If you say, "*Lā ilaha illĀllahu wahdahu lā sharīka lah, lahul mulku wa lahul hamdu wa huwa 'ala kulli shay 'in qadir*" to complete a hundred, your sins will be forgiven even if they are as abundant as the foam of the sea.

[Sunan Abi Dawud]

17: Dhikr Sayyidul Istighfar

A Qur'an memoriser can sin

A *Niqabi* can sin

A scholar can sin

An *Ustadh* can sin

No title or attire can protect us from sin because all the sons of Adam are sinners, but the best of sinners are those who repent often. Even if you are millions of steps away from Allah, remember that it only takes one step to return to Allah. When you come to Him walking, He will come to you running.

Imam an-Nawawi (Allah has mercy on him) said,

"Even if a sin is repeated a hundred or thousand times, if the slave repents sincerely, his repentance will be accepted."

[Syarh Muslim]

Prophet (peace be upon him) said:

"Allah will not tire of forgiveness unless you are tired of asking."

[al-Mu'jam al-Awsat]

Anas (May Allah be pleased with him) said:

I heard the Messenger of Allah (peace be upon him) saying, "Allah, the Exalted, has said: 'O' son of Adam! I shall go on forgiving you so long as you pray to Me and aspire for My forgiveness whatever may be your sins. O' son of Adam! I do not care even if your sins should pile up to the sky and should you beg pardon of Me, I would forgive you. O' son of Adam! If you come to Me with an earthful of sins and meet Me, not associating anything with Me in worship, I will certainly grant you as much pardon as will fill the earth."

[Ṣaḥiḥ at-Tirmidhi]

Prophet Muhammad (peace be upon him) said that the most superior request for forgiveness is the *Sayyidul Istighfar*. As stated in Ḥadith al-Bukhari, anyone who says that firmly believing in it and dies before the evening, or he/she says it in the evening, firmly believing in it and dies before the next morning, he/she will be from amongst the people of paradise.

Sayyidul Istighfar:

بِسْمِ اللّٰهِ الرَّحْمٰنِ الرَّحِيمِ

اَللّٰهُمَّ أَنْتَ رَبِّي لَا اِلَهَ إِلَّا أَنْتَ خَلَقْتَنِي وَأَنَا عَبْدُكَ وَأَنَا عَلَى عَهْدِكَ وَوَعْدِكَ مَا اسْتَطَعْتُ، أَعُوذُبِكَ مِنْ شَرِّ مَا صَنَعْتُ أَبُوءُ لَكَ بِنِعْمَتِكَ عَلَيَّ وَأَبُوءُ بِذَنْبِي فَاغْفِرْ لِي فَإِنَّهُ لَا يَغْفِرُ الذُّنُوبَ إِلَّا أَنْتَ

[Ṣaḥih al-Bukhari]

18: Nevertheless, They Persisted

Some people work better under pressure. Perhaps that is the reason why in their journey of personal growth, they tend to force themselves into enrolling in beneficial classes or volunteering in certain organisations, despite being busy at work or school or parenting. So that instead of browsing social media, they have to force themselves to do *hifz* (memorisation) revision because they are taking Qur'anic classes (for example).

To believe that you are extremely busy and have no time at all to invest in your individual development, especially spiritual growth, is quite self-victimising. True nobility of life lies in being superior to your former self.

For that, they voluntarily push themselves out of their comfort zone to form self-discipline. To stay focused. To make time when there is no time. To create two different routines. To stay out of anything that does not elevate them. They are exhausted. Nevertheless, they persisted. Indeed, rest is only for the dead.

"And that there is not for man except that [good] for which he strives."

[an-Najm, 53:39]

So yes. It might be stressful, but it is beautiful stress. Tiring, but a blessed kind of tired. Crazily hectic yet solemnly serene. Remember that all the difficulties will pass, but the rewards will remain forever. *In shaa Allah.*

Therefore, be inspired to do works of goodness that are not heavy so we can have consistency. For a little but continuous, is better than a lot which is interrupted.

'Abdullah ibn Mas'ud (may Allah be pleased with him) said,

"Indeed, I hate to see a man idle, not doing anything from the work of this life nor the Hereafter."

[Ḥilyatul Awliya']

19: Change of Hearts

Sometimes it is difficult to do *da'wah* to the people who are close to you because they know your past. They know whom you used to be, what you used to do and how you used to live. That alone is strong enough for them to refuse to listen and nullify what you believe to be haram now.

Please, do not use someone's past against them. You will be just reminding them of the mistakes they did back then. Try to read their facial expression carefully and understand the hurt in their eyes, every time you judge them by their past.

Ibn al-Qayyim said,

"Whoever mocks his brother for a sin he has repented from, will not die until he himself falls into the same sin."

Anyone can change at any time, with the *hidayah* (guidance) of Allah. *In shaa Allah.*

For that, we can no longer judge a person based on what others say. Hence, verifying news is a part of Islam. Get to know him, investigate his background, learn his personality, study his principles and evaluate his way of living life. If you keep relying on people's opinions, remember the same sun which melts the ice also hardens the clay. Their opinions may be true to you but not to others.

"And do not pursue that of which you have no knowledge. Indeed, the hearing, the sight and the heart—about all those [one] will be questioned."

[al-Isra', 17:36]

20: Real Manhood

A man said to his wife that he wants to love her like Prophet Muhammad (peace be upon him) loved Khadijah (may Allah be pleased with her). So, despite being already married, he continues to fast every Monday and Thursday as a way to protect his chastity from the *fitnah* (slander) of women outside. He refuses to attend reunions to avoid unnecessary mingles with *non-mahram* (marriageable) girls. He controls the way he carries himself around other females when she is not around. It is his loyalty through his action, not words—that gave her a sense of emotional security. *Alḥamdulillah*, for a husband like this.

Women are usually blamed for seducing men through the way she dresses or behaves. But history taught us that when Prophet Yusuf (peace be upon him) was seduced by Zulaikha, he managed to protect his chastity. This is real manhood.

In one of Ḥadith al-Bukhari, it was narrated that Prophet Muhammad (peace be upon him) was travelling on the road with his cousin, al-Faḍl ibn ʿAbbas and stopped to give verdicts. In the meantime, a beautiful woman from the tribe of Khathʿam came forward to ask him a question. The woman was very beautiful that al-Fadl could not help but stare at her. Seeing this, Prophet Muhammad (peace be upon him) held out his hand and turned his cousin's face away. [Ṣaḥiḥ al-Bukhari]

He did not tell the woman to cover her face. He did not tell her to hide. Instead, he averted his cousin's impolite stare.

> "Tell to the believing men to reduce [some] of their vision and guard their private parts."
>
> [an-Nur, 24:30]

Yes, it is easy to curse the 'Zulaikha' of our society, but have most men tried to be 'Prophet Yusuf' material? Verily, teaching our sons to lower their gaze is as important as teaching our daughters to cover up.

21: Be Mindful of Allah

It could be that a wife is endowed with numerous blessings by Allah because her husband is a man of *taqwa* (piety), As a wife, we sometimes wonder what good have we done that we are blessed in so many ways. Perhaps it is not us, maybe it is our husband.

Some husbands consistently pray *jama'ah* (congregational) in the masjid, and in return, their wives are blessed with good business or time to seek knowledge or ease in raising the kids. When a husband could not afford to give his wife everything she wants, Allah arranged it beautifully in such a way that his wife won a dress giveaway, or a friend sponsors their dream dinner or many other unexpected *rizq*.

It is in so many ways that Allah assists a husband in perfecting his responsibility to his wife because he is a man of faith. This matter is not only applicable to husbands who are responsible to their wives, but also to fathers, mothers, sons, daughters, and everyone mindful of the rights of Allah.

If we fulfil the rights of Allah, He will also help us to fulfil our rights—as a wife, daughter, sister, and many more. The blessings are extended to our family members and those who are close to us too. *In shaa Allah*! "Be mindful of Allah, and He will protect you." [Jami' at-Tirmidhi]

CHAPTER 2:
THE JOURNEY OF SEEKING HALAL *RIZQ*

"*Fear Allah and be graceful in seeking provision*"

[Sunan ibn Majah]

22: The Best Charity

Sometimes we go to work every day with low desire and claim very tired. Maybe we are not tired, we are just uninspired.

But did you know? In Islam, the money you spent on your family has a great reward, even greater than the money you spent for the sake of Allah or *sadaqah* to poor people!

"Of the dinar you spend as a contribution in Allah's path, or to set free a slave, or as a *sadaqah* given to a needy, or to support your family, the one yielding the greatest reward is that which you spent on your family."

[Ṣaḥih Muslim]

You work hard so you can pay for your house's bills, sustain your siblings' education, provide your family with healthy food, buy your parents the things they want—all of these are considered as the **BEST** charity in Islam.

Do not think that financially supporting our family is only a responsibility, because apparently, it is the best charity of all in the sight of Allah. On the Day of Resurrection, the salary from our work might be the reason for our shade.

"The believer's shade in the Day of Resurrection will be his charity."

[Jami' at-Tirmidhi]

So tell me, how can we not feel inspired?

Whenever you feel demotivated in working, remind yourself of this beautiful hadith and draw happiness from the promises of Allah.

May Allah grant our family benefit through us and bless us with *rizq* that will only bring us closer to Him. *Ameen.*

23: *Deen Over Money*

After four months of passing my professional licensure examination and on the verge of securing a job, I was finally called for an interview in one of the hospitals I had applied to. There were five panellists during the meeting and one of them asked me,

"Are you willing to take off your hijab during working hours in this hospital?"

I was shocked. Dr. X (also one of the panellists) then answered it on behalf of me, "Of course her answer will be no. I will not ask her that question because I am against this policy."

His courageous act of defending the dignity of his fellow Muslim sister touched my heart deep down to my arterioles. How can we ever violate our beliefs for money when we know Allah alone is the Provider of all kinds of Wealth? It was a sad fact that no matter how good you were, they would still discriminate against you just because you chose to be a practising Muslim.

Several months after that incident, to my amazement, I was offered a position in the government sector as a regional HIV/AIDS proficient. I was also invited to be a lecturer in a review centre during my off days. As if those were not enough, I was even hired by a private hospital to work during the weekend for on-call duties.

As I reminisce back on my struggle when I was jobless, I just see the bigger picture now. I was rejected by many hospitals because I defended to practise my Islamic rights while working, but anything you give up for the sake of Allah will return to you in a thousand times better state than when you had let it go! When we put our trust in Allah, He will surely direct us out in an unexpected way.

So I tell the future Muslim professionals and remind myself before others, to always put our trust in Allah. Never remove our hijab and never abandon our daily prayers for the sake of a job and money. If we refuse to leave something wrong for the fear of losing out on our wealth, we have doubted Allah's power to replace it with something much better for us in this world and the Hereafter. When we are offered money over *deen*, remember that Allah is *ar-Razzaq*.

"Do they not see that Allah extends provision for whom He wills and restricts [it]? Indeed, in that are signs for a people who believe."

[ar-Rum, 30:37]

24: On-Call Story

I remember, there was once during my on-call duty in a clinic that left a meaningful memory to me. It was not just a simple on-call day for me. The nurse in the clinic was very interested in Islam and asked me non-stop questions starting from hijab to boyfriend to dowry to polygamy and terrorism.

It just amazed me every time a stranger comes and simply asks anything about Islam, and it all began from their curiosity about the way we dress. When we don a hijab or grow a beard, we are displaying our faith publicly. Our characters, attitudes, and speech have become an unspoken *da'wah* to the community.

So, I advise myself before others, let us improve ourselves every day to be a better Muslim. To my sisters in Islam, know that hijab does not merely represent yourself but your religion as a whole. Let us wear it properly. The best way to defend Islam is to practise Islam correctly because it is never about preaching hard, it is reaching the heart.

"The best of you in Islam are those who are most excellent in character as long as you deeply understand the religion."

[Musnad Aḥmad]

Indeed, your profession is not what brings home your paycheck. Your profession is what you were put on Earth to help the *ummah* and spread the messages that it becomes spiritual in calling. Do not just be a professional, be a kind-hearted good practising Muslim professional.

25: His Story of Miracle

My husband brought me to a romantic dinner by the pool one night and during 'our date', he shared with me about his struggle back in his university days. It amazed me how I am still slowly getting to know my husband's life and just discovered another inspiring story about him.

He was an academic scholar of Northern Arizona University, USA, in mechanical engineering. Despite his scholarship, he still worked part-time as a student to have his own pocket money and to help ease the financial burden of his family back home. His dorm was merely a place to take a bath as most of the time he was outside studying or working.

Unfortunately, he lost his scholarship during his third year in which he had to pay for the tuition fees that cost him US$9000 per semester! *Alḥamdulillah*, his family could afford the payment so he was able to continue yet deep inside he was a bit demotivated. That feeling of you already did your best but your best was not good enough, and your only solution was to turn to Allah and ask for a miracle.

Verily, the magnitude of a sincere prayer during moments of desperation can be so powerful. Suddenly after two semesters, out of nowhere he received an unexpected award—a scholarship that recognises international students who successfully scored a pointer above 3.0 (highest is 4.0). When he saw the invitation, he had to pause for a while. He was shocked. He did not apply for it. He did not aware of it. He did not even know the existence of such an award! He described it as a 'miracle'. It was indeed a prayer, heard out of his desperation.

I must say, as a Muslim, the most fundamental idea that we must internalise is that *rizq* is in the hands of Allah—as one of the beautiful names of Allah (Glorified and Exalted is He) is *ar-Razzaaq*: The Provider, The Providence, The Supplier, The Bestower of Sustenance.

Allah (Glorified and Exalted is He) says:

"Allah extends the provision (*rizq*) for whom He wills and restricts [it]."

[ar-Ra'd, 13:26]

So remember always, to hand over your worries and put your trust in Allah as there is a strong connection between *taqwa* and *rizq*. As Allah (Glorified and Exalted is He) said,

"And whoever fears Allah—He will make a way out for him. And will provide for him from where he does not expect."

[at-Ṭalaq, 65:2-3]

26: Blessings In Disguise

My sister was offered a contractual position in the government sector, so she decided to quit her job in the private hospital she was working. But after four months only of working with the new job, they were informed that only one of them was able to have contract renewal for the following year as the government has a limited budget allocation.

She was devastated. After resigning from the former hospital and four months only of working in the new agency, suddenly she became jobless. No plan B. During that difficult period, I looked at her and said she did not deserve all of these. Just for the record, my sister ranked eighth place out of 2,400 examinees nationwide during the professional licensure examination. But we learned the hard way that academic excellence can be reduced to nothing in the real competitive world.

Nevertheless, being jobless was what forced her to apply for a permanent government position. "I'm just trying," she said. She submitted her resume passed the deadline, somehow unbelievably she was still called in for an interview. Knowing her co-applicants were among the best of the best, she almost gave up on attending the interview but she pushed herself to come and try her best anyway. "Just try.", she said.

Three months later, the result came out and unexpectedly she was hired! We could not describe how happy we were knowing that she would be working under the government for a regular employee position, compared to the previous position which was just contract-based.

Also, what we did not expect was, apparently, the previous government agency also rehired them back. They just delayed it for four months. Truly, if it was not because of the delay, my sister would never think of applying for the position she was currently hired. It took us some time later to see the whole scenario in a bigger picture and we realised that indeed when Allah take something away from His believers, He is just replacing it with something better. Witnessing the ups and downs of my very own sister, I would like to advise future young professionals:

1. NEVER GIVE UP

Even when things seem impossible, JUST TRY! The universe tends to fall in love with a determined heart.

2. TRUST ALLAH

I found myself guilty of thinking bad about Allah's plan. Always put your trust in Allah, that He will NEVER victimise His believers. Every delay is a redirection to a better opportunity and absolutely a blessing in disguise.

"And will provide for him from where he does not expect. And whoever relies upon Allah—then He is sufficient for him. Indeed, Allah will accomplish His purpose. Allah has already set for everything a [decreed] extent."

[at-Ṭalaq, 65:3]

27: Rizq After Nikaḥ

When I was single, I worked for three different companies—teaching, office, hospital—simultaneously. I had a stable job working with the government on weekdays; I accepted on-calls from a private hospital on the weekend and I was invited to teach during my off-days. My source of income comes from various directions. *Alḥamdulillah.*

As I was getting married, my greatest concern was to resign and give up all my careers to become a full-time housewife. I know my husband can sustain me, but there is a strong feeling of earning my own money.

Soon after our marriage, little did I know a door of *rizq* that I never saw coming has been opened for me. I applied for jobs in the translation industry and the very next day received an offer from a Singapore-based company. Amazingly, my income is even higher than what I used to earn in three companies altogether when I was single! In fact, I do not need to spend on transportation, food, and tax deduction. Since it is a working-from-home job, I am working while I can still do house chores at the same time. I travel a lot but I can still work anywhere since it is online. What is more interesting is, I am paid to read. This is the best job that suits my soul ever!

Truly, Allah knows best. I am speechless with the *qadr* of Allah. If there is one thing that I can advise the youth about marriage, then it would be:

> "And marry the unmarried among you and the righteous among your slaves and female slaves. If they are poor, Allah will enrich them from His bounty, and Allah is all-Encompassing and Knowing."
>
> [an-Nur, 24:32]

There is sustenance in *nikah* (marriage). Your wife, your children, and your family-in-laws can be your extra source of *rizq*. That is why when you are married you have more doors of *rizq* to be opened compared to being single.

But I would like to remind myself before others that *rizq* after marriage do not necessarily come in terms of monetary or cash or job. Most of the time, they come in the form of unexpected blessings and help in your moments of desperation.

So, get married for the sake of Allah and Allah will take care of your marriage. *In shaa Allah.*

28: Work Hard, Pray Harder

I did not request leave during vacation and still worked on the phone throughout my travel. I know some people who refused to take the day off despite being sick, some who still work during heavy rainy days, and some even volunteer to work during holidays due to the extra pay.

For people like us who are "no work, no pay" people, the more we work, the more the income. So as much as humanly possible, we try our best to maximise our earnings. At the end of the month, most people will only see the outcome but rarely noticed the sacrifices that we had to put up to.

I do believe that almost all of us, our hard-earned money was never spent only for ourselves, but on family and the people we loved. Deep inside, we know it is not our salary that makes us happy, it is our spending habit. You may not realise that your sincere sacrifices were driven by noble purposes.

Moreover, Muslims should develop a strong and responsible work ethic as Islam calls for hard work. We should do our best to provide for ourselves and others, rather than relying upon the charity of others.

Abu Hurayrah reported: The Messenger of Allah, (peace be upon him), said:

By him in whose hand is my soul, if one of you were to carry a bundle of firewood on his back and sell it, that would be better for him than begging a man who may or may not give him anything.

[Ṣaḥih al-Bukhari]

So, sacrifice if you have to. Never feel bad of keep accepting projects whenever there is an opportunity, or keep forcing yourself to work as long as there is strength. Perhaps it is through your sincerity and hard work, that Allah will keep blessing you abundantly so you can continue to be a blessing to others. Even the Prophet Dawud (peace be upon him) himself, would work with his own hands even though he was king of the Israelites.

Abu Hurayrah reported:

The Prophet, (peace and blessings be upon him), said:

"Dawud would never eat except from the earnings of his own hand's work."

[Ṣaḥih al-Bukhari]

However, in our pursuit of excellent professionalism, may we not forget our worship responsibility. Ustadh Halim

Hassan in his lecture said that there are two paths to seek *rizq*—*rizq* through working hard and *rizq* through *ibadah*.

The provision that Allah blesses the believers who work hard is different. It could be promotion or salary increase or great profit in business. On the other hand, the provision that Allah blesses the believers who perform acts of good deeds is also different. It could be in the form of obedient children or righteous spouses or beneficial friends and many more.

These paths are not the same for *rizq* comes in a different form. Therefore, it is not beneficial for a Muslim to say, "I will only work hard and neglect prayers," or vice versa. Rather, the best Muslim is the one who can combine these two paths. He works hard for halal income and at the same time, improves his religious worship (*sadaqah, istighfar, fasting,* and others) non-stop, seeking the unexpected *rizq* that Allah promised to the believers with *taqwa*.

> "And when the prayer has been concluded, disperse within the land and seek the bounty of Allah, and remember Allah often that you may succeed."
>
> [al-Jumu'ah, 62:10]

Work hard, pray harder!

29: The Blessed Income

In our journey of seeking the best job, may we constantly be reminded that there is no one perfect job. It could be that the boss is good but the salary is too small. It could be that the salary is good but the surroundings are toxic. It could be that your workmates are fun but you are away from your family. It could be that the job is full of happiness but it is not your course.

In the working world, we have to learn to accept imperfections and keep looking for positive aspects. A job is a job. It is a way to pay for your living, but that is it. Do not let work define your happiness. There is more to life than working.

My husband always reminds me that in asking for sustenance from Allah, do not ask for a high salary rather ask for a blessed income. Some people earn big money, but they are tested with constant problems that require constant spending of savings such as accidents, stolen belongings, repair of appliances, paying fines and many other problems. On the contrary, a low yet blessed income would suffice for an obedient Muslim as Allah would reduce his needs.

When you are asking something from Allah, see to it that the *du'a'* you are making will be beneficial to you both *dunya wal akhirah* (this world and hereafter). Do not just ask Allah to grant you a job so you will have a source of income, but ask Allah to make your job a means to be closer to Him. If you are asking to be promoted, follow it with the intention so you can be a better blessing to this *ummah* in the future. Even in worldly matters like dreaming of buying a fancy car like a Jaguar, do not just buy a Jaguar for the sake of buying a Jaguar, but make it as a *meaningful and beneficial Jaguar* by renewing your purpose that may this car ease your path to the masjid and to attend Islamic classes.

The beauty of Islam is that it does not restrict worshipping God to only praying, fasting and reading the Qur'an. It can encompass your daily actions simply through your intention. Remember, even a mundane routine such as brushing your teeth can be regarded as worship with the correct intention. So, keep renewing your intentions.

As 'Abdullah ibn Mubarak said:

"Perhaps a great deed is belittled by an intention.
And perhaps a small deed, by a sincere intention,
is made great."

In sha Allah, you will see the beauty of making *du'a'* in this manner. When He finally grant you a job, you will notice that you received not just a salary but He eases your way so you can make charity out of your little salary, *bi iznillah*.

All your wants that are halal are capable of bringing you closer to Allah. Everything that sounds *dunyawi* (worldly), can always be for the sake of *ukhrawi* (hereafter) when we correct our intention.

So, let us renew our intention that we go to work every day for the sake of Allah. Be thankful that we have a job, as Allah will add more unto those who are grateful. An increase in *ṣadaqah* as charity increases sustenance and protects wealth. May your hard work and my hard work be the kind of hard work that comes from a blessed source of *rizq*—that will only make us closer to Allah. *Ameen.*

30: The Foundation of *Rizq*

Accepting Eid money gifts on behalf of my nine-month-old son makes my heart ponder on the concept of *rizq* significantly—that even if you are just a baby and know not a single thing about this world—Allah has put aside your *rizq* for you.

That is why, Dr. Khalid Basalamah in one of his lectures has said that how come a man who works in a haram situation feel afraid to resign when Allah has provided him with *rizq* that makes him survive his childhood when he had no skills at all as a baby?

Shaykh Sulaiman ar-Ruhayli said if we want more *rizq*, then fear Allah. Want blessings in *rizq*? Fear Allah. Want continuous *rizq*? Fear Allah. This is because the foundation of *rizq* is fear of Allah.

> "And whoever fears Allah, He will make for him a way out and will provide for him from where he does not expect. And whoever relies upon Allah— then He is sufficient for him."

> [at-Ṭalaq, 65:2-3]

However, fearing Allah is not as simple as what the

tongue said. Fear of Allah is when you reject a position with a high salary because it deals with *riba'* (usury). Fear of Allah is when you were willing to remain jobless rather than working with hijab off. Fear of Allah is when you excuse yourself in the middle of an important meeting so you could perform *ṣalah*.

Fearing of Allah is *taqwa* and requires enormous courage to comply with what is against Allah's commands. But Allah says in the Qur'an,

> "And if the people of the cities had believed and feared Allah, certainly We would have opened upon them blessings from the heaven and the earth."

> [al-A'raf, 7:96]

31: Moderation In Spending and Giving

Wealth is in itself a test. Every God-conscious man knows that with great wealth comes great responsibility. Unlike the poor, a Muslim with wealth will be questioned about *zakat* (almsgiving), *ḥajj*, charity and family responsibility. So, wealth could be a blessing or a curse—depends on how someone handles his account. The best is to have one portion of the income for obligation expenses, one portion for savings, and another portion for charity. The percentage of each portion however depends on the individual's affordability.

However, it is just so sad to see how people tend to be judgmental when it comes to other people's financial management.

"He ate at a fancy restaurant. Isn't it better to feed a poor?"

"They went travelling. Why not sponsor a child to madrasah?"

Please, erase the condemnation of other people's budgetary.

They might be doing charity without other people knowing, and still afford to go out shopping for themselves. We usually see only the apparent.

"And they ask you what they should spend. Say, 'The excess [beyond needs]'."

[al-Baqarah, 2:219]

After the hard work, after the stress, after the overtime—I believe there is no harm in treating the soul for pleasure, as long as it does not involve forbidden extravagance.

"And [they are] those who, when they spend, do so not excessively or sparingly but are ever, between that, [justly] moderate."

[al-Furqan, 25:67]

"Keep some of your wealth for yourself, that will be better for you."

[Ṣaḥiḥ al-Bukhari and Muslim]

***Du'a'* for wealth and self-sufficiency:**

اللَّهُمَّ اكْفِنِي بِحَلاَلِكَ عَنْ حَرَامِكَ، وَأَغْنِنِي بِفَضْلِكَ عَمَّنْ سِوَاكَ

"O' Allah! Provide me with lawful (halal) livelihood, adequate to my needs instead of the unlawful (haram), and make me suffice with Your graces needing nothing from anyone else."

[Jami' at-Tirmidhi]

CHAPTER 3:
THE BEAUTY OF MARRIAGE

*"And We created you
in pairs."*

[an-Naba', 78:8]

32: Marry for *Deen*

In love, you cannot see the bad side of someone. That is the pathetic part of being in love. That sometimes even the worst person in this world can be the best person for your own belief. As McPaul said, "Love is not blind, it sees, but it doesn't mind". But the wise man thinks with his brain, not his desire, this is why men of *taqwa* marry for *deen* than beauty.

The Prophet (peace be upon him) said:

"A woman is married for four things: her wealth, her noble ancestry, her beauty and her religion. So win the religious woman; (otherwise) you will be a loser."

[Ṣaḥih al-Bukhari]

You may marry a woman for her beauty. You may marry her for her noble lineage. But if you are wise enough to prioritise what should be prioritised per the advice of the Prophet (peace be upon him), then you will marry a woman for her faith. Marry her for her devotion to Allah. Marry her for her *akhlaq*. Marry her because you know there is something in her, that you are unable to find in another. You will marry a righteous woman of your choice because it is in her womb that lies a generation of heroes, gallants, and the Qur'an preservers.

If we go back to the remarkable history of Islam, we will learn that among the bravest defenders of *deen* can be attributed directly to their mothers. Zubair ibnul 'Awwaam, the very first to unsheathe a sword in defence of the Prophet (peace be upon him), is a seed planted and nurtured by his mother, Safiyya bint Abdil Mutalib and an acute reflection of her.

You see, choosing a righteous spouse will not only influence you in your Muslim self-improvement journey. The decision you make today will create the future of the Islamic nation. Know that the woman you pursue is a reflection of you, your ambition, and your level of class. So choose your lady wisely, she represents you.

"A black and unattractive maid who is religious is better."

[Sunan ibn Majah]

What is beauty, if the faith is empty?

33: *Nikaḥ* is a Blessing

Do not be afraid to get married when you have all the means already. *Nikaḥ* is never a burden. It will not restrict your freedom. It will not stop you from travelling. It will not lessen your wealth. It will not shut you from seeking knowledge. It will not prevent you from serving your parents and siblings. Rather, *nikaḥ* is a blessing and every opportunity that comes after it only comes in a better version. A better life, a better career, better you. *In shaa Allah.*

Imam as-Saʻdi (Allah has mercy on him) said:

"Do not imagine that you will get poor if you marry. Allah incites towards marriage and promises richness after poverty."

[Taysir-ul-Karim]

So when the time has come for you to marry, do get married for the sake of Allah.

Abu Hurayrah reported:

The Messenger of Allah, (peace be upon him) said, "Verily, Allah will say on the Day of Resurrection: Where are those who love each other for the sake of my glory? Today, I will shelter them in my shade on a day when there is no shade but mine."

[Ṣaḥiḥ Muslim]

Marry to fulfil the Prophet's sunnah, marry for the glory of Islam. Some of us set certain requirements in looking for the perfect spouse not based on who he or she is, but what he or she has; such as nationality, professionalism, wealth, influence and so on so forth. Then we said this is for the betterment of *da'wah*. Really? Or are we just taking advantage of them in the name of religion for our purposes? Because to begin with, we never even love them for them and we did not marry them for who they are.

Allah's Messenger (peace be upon him) said,

"The reward of deeds depends upon the intention and every person will get the reward according to what he has intended. So whoever emigrated for Allah and His Apostle, then his emigration was for Allah and His Apostle. And whoever emigrated for worldly benefits or for a woman to marry, his emigration was for what he emigrated for."

[Ṣaḥiḥ al-Bukhari]

I believe, to be blessed with a 'brilliant package' partner

is a gift a bonus; not something we need to set for so we can take advantage of. I wonder what will happen when the time comes when Allah takes everything away from them except their faith, would we stay loyal to them? We fell in love with their flowers rather than their roots. So, when autumn came, we did not know what to do.

34: The Bridal Speech— Her Faith, His Destiny

Below was my speech during my wedding day on July 30, 2017:

"I know it is not traditional for a bride to give a speech during her wedding day, but today might be my last day to meet all of you since I will leave the Philippines tomorrow and settle down in Malaysia for good. So, I request the guests to please bear with me.

Firstly, I would like to thank all the guests who attended our special occasion today, especially my husband's family who flew all the way from Malaysia and Singapore. A wedding can happen anytime and anywhere but it can only be a true celebration with the presence of the people you love.

I think all of you had a glimpse of how my husband and I met. It was exactly almost a year ago when I received a message on Facebook from a stranger. It was a message from a mother, who was looking for a wife for her second son. I was shocked and I stalked her profile, learned that she only had six friends and we were not even connected on any social media. I thought she was just a scammer. However, guided with full *tawakkul* and continuous *istikharah* (prayer for seeking guidance), our relationship developed and today this stranger is officially my mother-in-law.

Up until this very day, I find it hard to explain to people that my mother-in-law just found me randomly on Facebook before recommending me to her son. Our love story seems so difficult to be comprehended by the logical thinking of a normal human being, but when it comes to destiny, there can be no mistake or coincidence. *Al-Qadr* is beyond the reasoning limitation of even the highest creature on Earth. My mother-in-law would simply reply, *"Ilham dari Allah"* (guidance from Allah) whenever people asked her how she found me.

To some people, they see our love story as a beautiful coincidence, to some of us we believed it is destiny. But to me, my husband is more than just a beautiful coincidence or destiny, he is a miracle. A gift of answered prayers.

A few months before I met my husband for our first *ta'aruf* (introduction), my mother left for *ḥajj* and I specifically asked her to make *du'a'* for me that if this man is good for me, may Allah make it easy. What can be more powerful than the *du'a'* of a mother, furthermore it is asked in the Holy Land of Makkah? The same goes with my mother-in-law, who asked for the perfect match for her son during the last ten days of Ramadan last year.

What can be more powerful than the *du'a'* made by a mother, during the nights of *Laylatul Qadr*? Perhaps it is the combination of *du'a'* by these sincere mothers and were heard in the Seven Heavens, that have helped us find each other, from the depths of the Peninsular sea across the mountains beyond the entire galaxies. *Allahuakbar*. I myself, have started to recite the *du'a'* for a righteous spouse at the age of seventeen. My husband is my ten years of *du'a'* which came true.

Today as I deliver this speech and stand side-by-side with my husband, I realised that he is not my childhood friend, not my classmate, schoolmate, or co-worker. He is not a mutual friend of friends and we are not even friends on Facebook. He is from the West, and I belong to the East. We never knew each other until nine months ago. But if someone is destined to be yours, at the perfect time surely Allah will direct him to you out of the crowd of seventy billion people on this Earth. Verily, nothing is impossible when it is fate.

I thought to finally finding my husband in an almost impossible way, would be the greatest surprise for me. But who would have expected, that fate slowly revealed that my very own sister will be my future sister-in-law? Verily, for the surprises from time to time, how can we deny the favours of the Lord? *Allahuakbar*.

To my husband, it has been twenty-four days of being your wife and you are amazing beyond my expectations. I love you so much, may Allah protect our marriage till *Jannah*."

Sincerely yours,

Aiyen Segovia

The Bride
July 30, 2017
Grand Astoria Hotel, Zamboanga City

35: Self-Betterment Through Marriage

When I was single, I told myself to look for an *'alim* (knowledgeable), *ḥafidhul* Qur'an (Qur'an preservers), professional, kind-hearted husband material so that I can be a better woman by having a husband with such criteria.

After being married for a while, my perspective towards the journey of self-betterment through marriage has changed and I realised how naive I was during those single years.

My husband is not a scholar from any Islamic university but he never gets tired of bringing me to circles of knowledge so both of us, can keep improving ourselves. He does not memorise the entire Qur'an but he bought me the best Qur'an set so I can pursue my Qur'an studies. He cannot teach me *nahu wa ṣarf* (Arabic grammar) but he searched for the best school in the city so I can continue learning. He takes care of our baby and the household chores just to give me some 'me time' at the corner of the room reading books. *Allahumma bariklahu!*

Honestly, because of him, I have improved a lot throughout our marriage even though he is not a scholar or a *ḥafidhul* Qur'an. My greatest realisation in this is that— does he put the effort in making you a better you? It is what truly matters. Putting in effort is a huge thing that makes a marriage work and helps you in improving yourself.

Instead of looking for a checklist of statuses, pray for the one who has the potential to consistently put effort into your journey of self-betterment because marrying someone who memorises the entire Qur'an but does not put any effort to help you in your Qur'an memorisation goals, then your perspective of 'ideal spouse' might be distorted.

Whether he is a scholar or an engineer, as long as he understands his religious duty to educate his family spiritually, is worth marrying.

"Our Lord, grant us from among our wives and offspring comfort to our eyes and make us an example for the righteous."

[al-Furqan, 25:74]

36: Partner to Heaven

The glory of a woman cannot be seen from 'with whom she is married to'. Had the glory of a woman been seen from her husband, then what about Maryam and Asiyah? What about the wife of Prophet Lut and Nuh?

This reminds me of powerful advice from our beloved *shaykh* back in those madrasah days when he said:

"To the single ladies, don't think that to seek knowledge of *deen* you must be married to an *'alim* with the expectation that he will teach you. Not every *'alim* can teach his wife. Some of the *'ulama* are very good in public speaking and *da'wah*, but not everyone has the consistency in teaching their wife for teaching requires skills, talent, passion and patience. Therefore, be independent in seeking knowledge and don't wait for anyone."

Anas ibn Malik reported:

The Messenger of Allah, (peace be upon him), said, "Seeking knowledge is an obligation upon every Muslim."

[Sunan ibn Majah]

It is not about the status, rather pray to have a partner who will be deeply interested in making you a better person. The one who invests seriously in his wife's spiritual growth, buy books and do things that will edify her and strengthen her walk with Allah, even though he himself is struggling.

I hope every believing woman will find a man as her partner to heaven. Together, they motivate each other in seeking knowledge for the rest of their lives. *Ameen.*

"The believing men and believing women are allies of one another."

[at-Tawbah, 9:71]

37: Rejoice Love Every Day

Some time ago last year, it was late evening and I thought we were just going to a supermarket for weekly grocery, so I was just in my pyjama and grabbed a random hijab plus cardigan.

To my surprise, after the grocery, my husband brought me right away to a fancy hotel for a romantic dinner night. Apparently, he already planned it and booked it earlier that day.

I was in my pyjama. I was shocked. I was not prepared.

That was one of the many crazy things my husband did on a random day to spoil his wife. The best part of celebrating your spouse without a special day is, you do not need to be prepared and the surprises now and then just increase your love towards each other.

We do not celebrate Valentine's but that does not mean we are being bitter or hate love. Rather, love is too powerful and for that, we always find ways to celebrate it every day.

In fact, love when celebrated for the sake of Allah is rewarded. *In sha Allah*. So keep loving your spouse every day. Make *du'a'* for your loved ones. Surprise your wife with a romantic dinner or a gift, as everything a husband spends on his wife for the sake of Allah will be rewarded.

Allah's Messenger (peace be upon him) said,

"You will be rewarded for whatever you spend for Allah's sake even if it were a morsel which you put in your wife's mouth."

[Ṣaḥih al-Bukhari]

Revive the *sunnah*, and leave what is not from the teaching. Keep up the good faith, and spread love only for the sake of Allah.

38: Be the Water In a Fire

I recall the night when we arrived in Tokyo from Kyoto, Japan, and we got lost because the guesthouse owner gave us the wrong address. It was already midnight and the weather was freezing! I was hungry and tired. My arm was painful because I had been carrying my five-month infant on my shoulder for hours. My patience was thinning even more because the owner could not be contacted and worse, the taxi driver left us at the roadside.

I was getting angry, upset, and frustrated. I felt like I wanted to shout. Amazingly, my husband maintained his calmness despite my spoiled mood. He managed to remain composed under pressure despite the tense circumstances. He calmly searched for the guesthouse one by one while I was standing at the corner of the road, freezing and kept saying '*astaghfirullāh*' so Allah would give us a way out of our distress.

Alḥamdulillah, it took my husband around ten minutes to look for the correct house. After Allah, he did it on his own without my help, not even the guesthouse owner. This was the power of remaining calm in seeking a solution, you should not panic. You solved a problem, and you saved your relationship. A lesson learned for me.

Every time I remember that memorable night, I always feel proud of him. The key to a harmonious relationship is to be calm when one is angry.

"If your spouse is angry, you should be calm. When one is fire, the other should be water."

['Umar ibn al-Khattab (may Allah be pleased with him)]

When Imam Ahmad ibn Hanbal's wife passed away, he said, "*WAllahi* I lived with her for forty years and we did not argue once." He was asked 'How?' He said, "Whenever she gets upset and tries to argue, I stay quiet. And whenever I'm upset and try to argue, she stays quiet."

39: The Unspoken Sacrifices

In life, sometimes we practice selective secrets for the benefit of others. We opted not to complain to the people we love no matter how hard it is because we do not want them to worry. The same goes for me and my husband. Due to his work commitment, we only meet once or twice a month most of the time. I know he hides a lot about the danger of his work because he does not want me to worry, the same way I would struggle on my own on some things at home without telling him so he will not be stressed out at work. We can only talk to Allah during those moments of difficulty.

"I only complain my suffering and grief to Allah."

[Yusuf, 12:86]

Therefore, in marriage, it is not benefiting for a husband to think his wife does not do much just because she stays home all day, neither does it benefits a wife to think that her husband does not do much in taking care of the children because he is at work all day. In all honesty, it is only when we are in our spouse's shoes and try to do what they do daily that we will realise they have been doing a lot in silence.

Likewise,

to fathers who endure massive workloads,

to mothers with house chores overload,

to daughters and sons who are working abroad,

to all the people who keep saying they are fine even when they are not,

those who chose to remain silent about their struggles because they do not want their loved ones to be sad,

May Allah reward you abundantly for your unspoken sacrifices and give credit to you when credit is due. *Ameen.*

"Conceal hardship so much so that people presume
you are blessed and have an easy life."

[Imam ash-Shafi‘e (Allah has mercy on him)]

A *du‘a’* that can be recited,

رَبِّ إِنِّي لِمَا أَنزَلتَ إِلَيَّ مِن خَيرٍ فَقِيرٌ

"My Lord, indeed I am, for whatever good
You would send down to me, in need."

[al-Qaṣaṣ, 28:24]

40: Romanticism

I remember the night when I was still pregnant with my first son, I already cooked for dinner but I did not feel like eating it so I asked my husband to eat out but then we kept moving from one restaurant to the other because I just really did not feel like eating any of the food. There were times when I was in dilemma—Set A or B, and eventually, I ordered set A while my husband ordered set B so I could taste both, though I know he really wanted set C.

Many times, husbands thought that romanticism is in the idea of bringing their wives to a sweet dinner night. But honestly, those little moments when you sacrifice your wants to fulfil the demand of your wife's crazy appetite; or switch plate with her when you noticed she silently regretted her choice of food and preferred yours; or when you wake up in the middle of the night because your wife is craving for ice-cream; or simply be patient with her when she did not finish her food and you even helped her eat all her leftovers. These acts are generosity in their sincerest form, love in its purest form.

I know some men thought they can easily handle a woman, but wait until you marry and live with a woman named 'wife'. You will be truly tested. Despite all of that, be patient with her because she is your greatest blessing. You may have loving parents, supportive friends, obedient children but when you grow old, it is your spouse who will wake up by your side and still listen to all your corny jokes.

"And of His signs are that He created for you from yourselves mates that you may find tranquillity in them; and He placed between you, affection and mercy. Indeed, in that are signs for a people who give thought."

[ar-Rum, 30:21]

41: Keep It Halal

Perhaps my greatest achievement in life was when I decided to accept the wedding proposal of my husband, whom I just met once before marriage. Through him, Allah bestowed upon me an abundance of provision and happiness. I gave up on my medical career for him but through him, I found my current profession which until today still renders me speechless with the unexpected *rizq*. I left my family far away for him but through him, I am blessed with two children as my extreme bundle of joy. Through him, my dream to travel the world came true. Through him, my Islamic faith has improved a lot. *Allahumma bariklahu.*

In Islam, marrying someone whom we barely know does not mean we just blindly select a partner for life. Rather, we do our part first then rely upon Allah. Among the getting married efforts are to be open to *shariah*-compliant matchmaking, do *istikharah*, make sincere *du'a'*, perform *tahajjud*, conduct *ta'aruf* and thorough background investigation then lastly, *tawakkul*.

Anas ibn Malik reported:

A man said, "O' Messenger of Allah, should I tie my camel and trust in Allah, or should I leave her untied and trust in Allah?" The Prophet, peace and blessings be upon him, said, "Tie her and trust in Allah."

[Jami' at-Tirmidhi]

Most importantly, guard your heart against *fitnah* throughout the deciding process as everything you do flows from it. Keep the pre-marital relationship halal, make the *nikaḥ* intention pure.

"And do not approach unlawful sexual intercourse. Indeed, it is ever an immorality and is evil as a way."

[al-Isra', 17:32]

For that, I pray every woman with a good heart will remain patient in waiting for the good hands of the man destined for her—the man who will bring her *abundance of provision and happiness*.

"Good women are for good men, and good men for good women."

[an-Nur, 24:26]

42: The Love Letter

If a stranger has bravely come to propose to you, how will you know he is the one for you, without dating? How can you know he is a good man and you are compatible, without chatting or calling?

First, pray *istikharah*. Allah will make it easy for you if it is already written that he is the one. As Muslims who believed in *qadr* and fate, we know that Allah has written our soulmate's name fifty thousand years before the Earth was created, before the sky was introduced to the moon, and before the Sun met the sea.

'Abdullah 'Amr ibn al-'As reported:

I heard Allah's Messenger (peace be upon him) as saying: "Allah ordained the measures (of quality) of the creation fifty thousand years before He created the heavens and the earth, as His Throne was upon water."

[Ṣaḥih Muslim]

Secondly, conduct a background investigation. Reach out to his friends and family, know his personality and other important information. One powerful piece of advice that I have learned from Ustadh Dr. Syafiq Basalamah in one of his lectures, was to never ask about a man's *akhlaq* (manners) through the *masjid*. It could be that he may be a man who always prays in the first row during prayers, but outside he is a man who never pays his debt even when he has the means to. That is why 'Umar al-Khattab (may Allah be pleased with him) said, you do not know someone until you live with him, travel with him or do money transactions with him.

So, to the single ladies who are doing background investigation about the man she is going to marry, you should ask what the man does beyond the masjid. Inquire his family members how he behaves at home, a friend who travelled with him before or someone who lends or borrows money from him.

The third is *ta'aruf*. Let him meet you and your family, exchange personal insights. The man you choose to be your partner affects everything in your life. Your faith, your mental health, your happiness, how you raised your children and many more. So before accepting a marriage proposal, you should give justice to yourself by doing your best in decision-making then leave the rest to Allah.

"Then when you have taken a decision, put your trust in Allah. Certainly, Allah loves those who put their trust in Him."

[Ali 'Imran, 3:159]

As for my husband and I, after these three, we also decided to write a letter but turned out to be a book because a piece of paper was not enough. The book was dedicated to one another and we exchanged it after ta'aruf. His book for me was handwritten, making it look even more sincere and contained everything that the heart wants to say to the future spouse. He said something about himself, his *aqeedah* (creed), his vision and mission in marriage, his strengths and weaknesses, his expectation of his future spouse and many more. Just like a resume!

Alhamdulillah, today he is my husband and it feels great to re-read his CV of 'application-to-be-your-husband' for me. A black and white document to remind him of his manifestos and promises before marriage, why we got married in the first place, how I captured his heart, why he wants me to be the mother of his children, and many more.

If you are married, take a little time today and remember the moment you knew your spouse was the one for you. It is fun to go down memory lane, reminiscing about your love story. Also, make sure you express your love frequently and sincerely.

"Women like attention and they like to be told clearly that they are loved. So do not be stingy in expressing your love for your wife. If you become limited in expressing your love, you will create a barrier of harshness between you and her, and there will be a decrease in affection."

[Imam Aḥmad ibn Ḥanbal (Allah has mercy on him)]

43: My Man

This man invented the fastest robot in the world at the age of thirteen in Yokohama, Japan. This man was the only Asian in the research team manufacturing a component for a NASA spaceship in Florida, USA. Even today, this man has designed many types of equipment for big companies such as Halliburton and Aerospace.

And this man is my man, who helps me clean the toilet at our home. A chauffeur to everyone when he is back to his mother's house. A plumber. A babysitter. A cook helper. A cleaner. This man is a man whom everyone can depend on when he is around.

Extraordinary intelligence may capture the world's attention, but it is a kind heart that captures many hearts.

As the Messenger of Allah said,

"The most complete of the believers in faith is the one with the best character. And the best of you are those who are best to their women."

[Jami' at-Tirmidhi]

I keep some pictures of him doing house chores and taking care of the family that I took in secret, to remind myself that I must be grateful. To overlook his little weaknesses and ponder upon his many kindnesses. Indeed, this man is my man. The King of our kingdom, the Prince of my heart.

44: A Child to His Wife

Whenever I eavesdrop on my husband's conversation on the phone discussing work, it suddenly reminds me of how smart he is. Probably because at home he acts like a big baby, sometimes he is even jealous of the extent of attention I give to our children as compared to him. But outside, especially at the workplace, I see his leadership and maturity. It is like seeing two different personalities.

But I believe, in the teaching of the Islamic faith, men are supposed to be like that. They should be easygoing and cheerful with their wife. *Allahumma bariklahu.*

"A man should be like a child with his wife, but if she needs him, he should act like a man."

['Umar ibn al-Khattab (may Allah be pleased with him)]

45: A Grateful Wife

That moment when he kneels to put her shoes on. When he carries her bag every time they are out to make sure it is safe. When he let her into the inner part every time they walk on the street to protect her. When he brings home some food for her every time after work. When he reminds her of *ḍuḥa* (morning supplementary prayer) every morning and *Surah al-Kahfi* every Friday.

Sometimes, it is not really about bringing her to a fancy restaurant, buying her a Tissot watch or sponsoring her a trip abroad. It is always the little things that make an ordinary man an extraordinary husband.

I believe every husband is extraordinary in his little way. It takes a grateful wife to see these little things on an everyday basis. May Allah grant us hearts that appreciate the unnoticed effort by our spouse and make us among the contented. *Ameen.*

The Prophet (peace be upon him) said:

"I was shown the Hell-fire and that the majority of its dwellers were women who were ungrateful." It was asked, "Do they disbelieve in Allah?" (or are they ungrateful to Allah?) He replied, "They are ungrateful to their husbands and are ungrateful for the favours and the good (charitable deeds) done to them. If you have always been good (benevolent) to one of them and then she sees something in you (not of her liking), she will say, 'I have never received any good from you.'"

[Ṣaḥih al-Bukhari]

46: An Open Letter to the Future Married Couples

The beginning of a marriage is very sweet, but it is very crucial. It is the period where you and your spouse start a new life together and decide what kind of laws you would like to implement in your new little family. Whatever house rules that you both have implemented when there were just the two of you, will become your family's habit for a lifetime when you have children.

To the couples who are getting married soon, set your religious relationship goals as early as now and implement them right after *nikah*. It could be the recitation of the Qur'an every after *fajr*, or as simple as no eating and drinking while standing.

But be careful of what we implement. Sometimes, we are "romanticising Islam" when we say, "I want my husband to be my five times prayer imam" when in fact, a Muslim man should perform his five times prayers in the masjid and be a *makmum*.

Also, whatever *sunnah* that you have been practising since you were single, carry it on even until you are married and invite your spouse to do the same. My husband, for example, has been practising Monday and Thursday fasting and he still carries it on even after marriage and encourages me as well. It is sweeter now as he has a wife to cook *sahur* for him as compared to when he was single, living alone who only had water for *sahur*.

The-bottom-line:

1. Marriage is a great door to *Jannah*, so make the best out of it. You marry one another with the intention that *I will try to bring this person to Paradise with me.*

2. Practise *sunnah* together with your spouse right after *nikah*, so it will become a consistent habit in your future family.

3. Help each other. Strive hard to attain the love of Allah so He will put more love between you and your spouse.

"The believing men and believing women are allies of one another. They enjoin what is right and forbid what is wrong and establish prayer and give zakat and obey Allah and His Messenger."

[at-Tawbah, 9:71]

CHAPTER 4: THE ROAD TO PARENTHOOD

"To Allah belongs the dominion of the heavens and the earth; He creates what He wills. He gives to whom He wills, female [children], and He gives to whom He wills, males. Or He makes them [both] males and females, and He renders whom He wills barren. Indeed, He is Knowing and Competent."

[ash-Shura, 42:49-50]

47: A Gift from Heaven

When I was first informed about the presence of another life in my body, I was extremely happy. Throughout the pregnancy period, I had to suffer months of unexplained discomfort due to hormonal changes and my husband had to increase his patience beyond the limit. Nine months of pregnancy was a roller-coaster ride.

But it was the existence of that tiny heartbeat in my womb that gave us the privilege to be prioritised in this world. People from the grocery shop, airport, government offices, and the public also have treated me with extra care and VIP treatment. The manifestation of our child in my womb, although not born yet, have already elevated our status in this world. I wonder what more in the hereafter when *Paradise lies under the feet of your mothers.*

I recall an event in an airport where I was seven months pregnant. Upon arrival, there were hundreds of people falling in line for immigration purposes. We were at the back of the queue when suddenly, an immigration officer came to us and invited us to come forward. She offered me to sit on a couch and took away our passports for processing. I felt honoured and happy for being able to cut the long lines and my husband was able to tag along as well. We got the privilege due to the 'intercession' of our not-yet-born baby. Indeed, he is a gift from Heaven.

While waiting comfortably for our passports, I watched the lines where hundreds of people were still anxiously waiting for their turn. This is in *dunya*. Can you imagine what the Day of Resurrection would be like where all of us will be gathered and hoping for intercession?

It is said on the Day of Resurrection, we will be gathered naked, barefooted as well as uncircumcised and the first human being to be dressed will be Prophet Ibrahim (peace be upon him).

"The first person to be dressed on that day will be Prophet Abraham."

[Ṣaḥih al-Bukhari]

It is also said that during that Day, all of us would be standing only a mile away from the sun and hence some of us will even sink into their perspiration till their mouths!

"The sun will be a distance of a mile from the creation on the Day of Resurrection. People will sink in their perspiration according to their deeds. Some would sink in their perspiration till their ankles, while others would sink in it to their thighs and waists; yet others would sink in it till their mouths!"

[Ṣaḥih Muslim]

It is also said that we will stand there for fifty thousand years long, waiting for the decision.

"That day will be fifty thousand years long, after which a person will be admitted into Paradise or cast into Hell."

[Sunan Abi Dawud]

SubḥanAllah! May Allah grant us an easy reckoning!

Du'a' for easy reckoning:

اَللّٰهُمَّ حَاسِبْنَا حِسَابًا يَّسِيْرًا

Oh Allah, grant me an easy reckoning.

[Musnad Aḥmad]

48: A Woman's Jihad

Women are complicated creatures and will become even more complex when they are pregnant. In the matter as simple as food, some have cravings while some have an aversion. Some cannot even eat certain brands of rice. It is in unexplainable moments like these, all they need is understanding and support from people they love the most. We have to learn to be sensitive to their feelings and acknowledge their emotional struggles.

Even the greatest man in the history of mankind, Prophet Muhammad (peace be upon him), was very sensitive and gave high appreciation to women's feelings such that he along with the *sahabah* delayed their travel in one of their important journeys, just to help A'isha (may Allah be pleased with her) searched for her lost necklace. [Ṣaḥiḥ al-Bukhari]

It was on January 29, 2018, when I found out that I was pregnant with my firstborn. My nine months pregnancy was like a roller-coaster ride. I went through forty weeks of non-stop body changes. I was borderline with Gestational Diabetes Mellitus (GDM) during my first trimester, got infected with chickenpox during the second trimester, and suspected Carpal Tunnel Syndrome (CTS) during the third trimester. Not to mention the morning sickness, leg cramps, weight gain, and many more.

For every calamity that befallen my weak pregnant body due to suppressed immune system or hormonal overload, I recited the *du'a'* from Umm Salamah intending to seek reward and easy delivery as replacement of the pain.

$$إِنَّا لِلهِ وَإِنَّا إِلَيْهِ رَاجِعُونَ$$

"To Allah we belong and to Him is our return. O' Allah, reward me for my affliction and replace it for me with that which is better."

[Ṣaḥih Muslim]

It is said that a woman was a fighter in Allah's way from the time she became pregnant up to the time she delivered. If she died during delivery, her position would be that of a martyr.

The Prophet (peace be upon him) said:

"The woman who dies in pregnancy or childbirth is a martyr."

[Sunan Abi Dawud]

Alḥamdulillah, I delivered a healthy baby boy weighing 4.35kg at 12.33 pm on September 29, 2018. All the pains were worth it, the moment I heard my baby cry, the very first time I saw him, the second I hold him in my arms. No words in the world can ever picture that magical moment of giving birth. It is a miracle to think how absolute perfection can come out of a human body. *Allahuakbar*!

To all pregnant women, just bear a little more patience. All the sufferings will be replaced with explosive happiness on the day you meet your little ones. *In sha Allah.*

49: The Islamic Responsibility of a Mother

They said, when you educate a woman, you educate a generation. So, let us have that ambition to be the first to teach our children how to recite the Qur'an and perform *salah*. Teach them *al-Fatihah*, it will be a part of their prayers for life. Grab that opportunity, as what profession can be compared to being a mother?

Paradise is believed to be under her feet.

[Sunan ibn Majah and Nasa'i]

Indeed, the woman is the backbone of a family as is said,

"Behind every great person, there is a woman in whose home they were raised."

[A Woman's Guide to Raising a Family pp. 19-20, Shaykh Ṣalih al-Fawzan]

"The mother is the first school. If she is righteous, the progeny becomes righteous."

[Fath-ur-Rabb al-Wadud (2/256), Shaykh Aḥmad an-Najmi]

"Every mother is a da'iyah (caller to Islam for her child/family)."

[The Islaamic Awakening pp. 223-229,

Shaykh Ṣalih ibn Uthaymin]

The best way to have righteous children is to try to be righteous parents, too. We cannot teach what we do not do or know for that matter. It is hard to raise strong children when we ourselves are broken adults that needed to be repaired too. But the beauty of planting the seeds of faith in our children is, we can reap the rewards even when we are already in the grave! So, parenting according to Islamic guidelines might be the hardest but it could be the most rewarding *in sha Allah*.

"It is upon the parents to teach their children, the young ones, first things first—*tawḥid* (unification of Allah). When the child can distinguish the good and bad, he is taught the *wuḍu'* (ablution) and the prayer, and he is warned against fornication, stealing, lying, and others. When he is mature, then what the Pen wrote comes to pass."

[Imam Shamsuddin Muhammad ibn Aḥmad ibn

Uthman ad-Dhahabi]

Supplication to have good children:

رَبِّ هَبْ لِي مِن لَّدُنكَ ذُرِّيَّةً طَيِّبَةً ۖ إِنَّكَ سَمِيعُ الدُّعَاءِ

"My Lord, grant me from Yourself a good (pure) offspring. Indeed, You are the All-Hearer of invocation."

[Ali 'Imran, 3:38]

50: The Glory of Motherhood

My husband left me for work when I was only eight days post-partum. I usually never cry when he goes offshore, but that day I had a mental breakdown and wept my heart out. Not because I was going to miss him, but more on being terrified with all the responsibilities thrown on my shoulder without him being by my side.

My body was very weak but I have to force myself to get up in the middle of the night and feed my new-born; my surgery wound was still fresh but I had to drive to the hospital twice a day for ten days straight for my heparin injection; I could barely walk but I needed to bring my son to the clinic for fourteen days for his jaundice monitoring. I was both in pain and extremely fatigued. It was only when I became a mother myself, that I finally understood the magnitude of strength that motherhood demands.

All of these were an eye-opener to me. I am fortunate because my husband only goes away for a week or two now and then. But how about those mothers with husbands who work abroad and come home only once a year? What about mothers with irresponsible or abusive husbands? What about single mothers?

Yet we learned how single mothers raised the most

influential people in the Islamic nation. The mother of Imam Bukhari was a single mother. The mother of Imam Shafi'e was a single mother. Even the mother of Prophet Muhammad (peace be upon him), Aminah bint Wahb, was a single mother. *Allahuakbar.*

I guess when a woman becomes a mother, all of the sudden she has an extraordinary kind of strength as her 'superpower' that no matter the pain, no matter the hardship, no matter the hurt, no matter the bruises—as long as it is for the sake of her children, she will forever say *I got this* even with tears in her eyes.

The sad part is, we rarely know her battles because she went to war in silence. Honestly, with what price do we pay for the glory of motherhood? May Allah grant them *Jannatul Firdaus.*

Du'a' for parents:

رَّبِّ ارْحَمْهُمَا كَمَا رَبَّيَانِي صَغِيرًا

"My Lord, have mercy upon them as they
brought me up (when I was) small."

[al-Isra', 17:24]

51: The Power of a Mother's Prayers

It is astonishing to think that when you have become a mother, every word that comes from your mouth for your children will be a *du'a'* that is heard up to the seven heavens. Even the lyrics of your self-composed lullaby, have the power to change the destiny of your children.

The founder and the first caliph of the Umayyad Caliphate, Mu'awiyah ibn Abi Sufyan, became a leader of the entire Muslim nation due to his mother's *du'a'*. When Mu'awiyah was still a child, his mother, Hind bint Utbah, heard someone say, "If he goes on to become a man, he will lead his community." She responded, "May I lose him if he will only lead his people!" And indeed, he ended up leading the entire Muslim nation. In fact, when needing to identify himself, he would proclaim: "I am the son of Hind!"

Therefore, let us as mothers make it a habit that only good words come out of our mouths for our children, even during our moments of anger or disappointment.

Just like Imam Adil Kalbani, whose mother would always say, "May Allah guide you! And make you the imam of the Ka'bah!" whenever she is angry at him. So Allah answered her *du'a'* and he went on to become the Imam of the Ka'bah!

"Three supplications will not be rejected by Allah SWT—the supplication of the parent for his child, the supplication of the one who is fasting, and the supplication of the traveller."

[Jami' at-Tirmidhi]

I want my sons to know that when the time comes and maybe I am no longer on this Earth, perhaps they will always find it is easy in this life to memorise the words of Allah and act upon it, is probably because the *du'a'* of their mother. *In sha Allah.*

For there are two things in this world that will never leave them—Allah and their mother's *du'a'*.

"Abubakr Siddique,

Ummi's good son,

Ummi's son who's ṣalih,

Ummi's clever son,

Who'll be a ḥafidhul Qur'an when he grows up."

52: My Wonderful VBAC Experience

My firstborn was delivered through a C-section and it was less than a year before I was confirmed pregnant again. Our mindset was actually to go for another caesarean procedure, but our hearts just followed the flow—natural or caesarean—Allah would only give the best.

Alhamdulillah, it was just exactly a few hours before my appointed admission for caesarean surgery, that my water broke and I felt intense contraction already. I almost broke my husband's arms while enduring the excruciating pain. Three hours after that, *Alhamdulillah,* I gave birth to another healthy baby boy weighing 3.12kg through normal delivery.

Indeed, every birth story is unique.

The magnitude of pain I suffered throughout the contraction was the greatest pain I have experienced in my life; the strength that I had as my husband was there to hold my hand during my 'push' moment; the thankfulness upon seeing him cry as he saw our baby was out safely while I almost lost my breath; the deep affection to hear him said "I love you so much" after having him witnessed one of human greatest sacrifices ever existed…

…were among the beautiful gifts that wrapped inside my vaginal birth after a caesarean (VBAC) wonderful adventure, which I think I would not have experienced should I undergone surgery.

Verily, our lives are filled with things that we think are mere coincidences but they are messages from Allah to rectify and beautify our path in life. May Allah increase us in *taqwa*, for every plan that went better than expected.

"But they plan, and Allah plans. And Allah is the Best of Planners."

[al-Anfal, 8:30]

To our second son, Umar Farooque,

"May Allah make you a blessing for your parents and a blessing for the *ummah* of Muhammad (peace be upon him)."

(*Du'a' for newborns*; Imam al-Tabarani)

53: Siddique and Farooque

I remember finding out I was pregnant with Abubakr Siddique and went shivering because I was extremely happy.

And I remember exactly how it felt when the doctor laid Umar Farooque on my chest for the first time, all fidgety and perfect.

But being a mother is the hardest job on the planet. You can have a wonderful and memorable day with your children but still have moments when you question your sanity, moments when you question your capacity, moments that crush you.

So I tell myself;

If every time your day did not go as you planned, do not worry. You are not doing it wrong, it is just that hard. If you cry because you are too hungry and your baby did not want to let go of his milk, do not worry. You are not doing it wrong, it is just that hard. Remember, no mother is doing it wrong. Motherhood is just naturally hard.

But I keep telling myself too;

That it is easy to get caught up in the daily toils of motherhood. But when you stop for a moment and look around at your life, you have everything you have always wanted. Your life could have gone in a hundred different directions. Instead, here you are, getting to be the mother of these two. The fact remains that this beautiful, exhausting, wonderful season of parenting young children is the greatest privilege you have ever had.

> "We have enjoined upon man, to his parents, good treatment. His mother carried him with hardship and gave birth to him with hardship, and his gestation and weaning [period] are thirty months."
>
> (al-Aḥqaf, 46:15).

54: Knowing Allah Through Motherhood

I have never witnessed Allah's Majesty like that in the development and growth progress of a baby. Those miracle moments when he smiled for the first time; when he rolled for the first time; when he finally could speak his first word; his ability to crawl, walk and run; his ability to express his emotion; all of which are non-teachable and only come in God's perfect timing. I observed how their body changed and how they gained weight, all from my breastmilk—their food directly from God through me.

I held my babies during their Day One on Earth, all weak and fragile. But day after day, I watched them evolve from weakness to strength. Claiming the truthfulness of Allah's words in the Qur'an,

> "Allah is the one who created you from weakness, then made after weakness strength, then made after strength weakness and white hair. He creates what He wills, and He is the Knowing, the Competent."
>
> [ar-Rum, 30:54]

My second son Umar Farooque is three months old now as I am writing this piece. *Allahumma bariklahu.* Observing him develops naturally with his food and baby skills totally under the care of Allah, shows how powerless I am as a mother and taught me another level of submission to Allah.

Verily, He is the Most Knowing of us, even when we were still in our mother's womb. How can we ever find another care greater than the care of our Lord?

"He was most knowing of you when He produced you from the earth and when you were foetuses in the wombs of your mothers."

[an-Najm, 53:32]

55: Motherhood Getaway

My husband gifted me with a 3D2N stay in a hotel to let me have some alone time because I was taking some exams soon. He printed for me all the books that I needed and let me check in to a hotel so I could focus on reviewing, while he would take care of our son and other house chores back at home.

As a direct breastfeeding mother, I have never been detached from my son for more than three hours since he was born even though I am working and studying. He tagged along in all of my work meetings and online classes. To be away even for just one night will be a great challenge for all of us. I thanked my husband for this 'sacrifice'.

Indeed, having a life partner who continually invests in your personal growth and motivates you to do better in life, makes you realise that a relationship is more than just falling in love. Marriage is more than just growing old together; it is also about growing in faith together, achieving worldly and *akhirah* goals together. Women glow differently and turn out to be the best version of themselves when they are loved the right way.

The three days two nights stay in a hotel also served as my 'motherhood getaway', where after such a long time, I finally got some alone time. Reviving that feeling of 'being single' again. Having a peaceful eight hours of sleep. Going shopping hands-free. But I realised the 'mom-cation' was more on switching of roles with him.

I finally understood how lonely it feels to return to an empty hotel with no laughter and noise, I also wished to have an hourly update about what is happening at home. This is what he felt when he had to go to the ocean for weeks or months, especially those areas with no Internet at all. Meanwhile, I also hoped my husband had a glimpse of my daily tasks and what is it like to be a full-time housewife while working and studying, not to mention direct breastfeeding.

When we were finally back in each other's arms again, somehow the magnitude of gratefulness increased. Verily, it is only when we are in our spouse's shoes and tries to do what they do daily that we will realise—apparently, they have been doing a lot, in silence. May we be more compassionate, more merciful and gentler towards our spouses and family members.

Ka'b reported:

Allah Almighty said to Moses, upon him be peace, "O' Moses, be soft in nature, for the most abhorred creation to me is one within whom is arrogance, in whose tongue is sharpness, and in whose heart is hardness. The most beloved character traits to me are mercy, compassion, kindness, and gentleness. O' Moses, be merciful to my creation and I will have mercy on you. O' Moses, I am merciful and I love those who are merciful. Blessed are those who are merciful. Again, blessed are those who are merciful. And again, blessed are those who are merciful."

[Ḥilyatul Awliya']

56: The 'Underrated' Dads

Later in marriage when you hit parenthood, you will realise what you wish for in your spouse is not big money or a 'six-pack'. A pretty face and a good bank account are nice to have but at the end of the day, there are so much more you should be looking for.

At 2 a.m. when your newborn is crying, but you are extremely tired and weak for postpartum, you will be hoping for a caring husband who will let you rest and let him take over. It seems like a small deed, but trust me, it will mean the world to you. During a crucial time like that, it will not be how he looks or what he owns that matters.

I remember, when I was suddenly admitted to the hospital for labour, my husband had to juggle between work and taking care of me, all alone by himself because we have no family in Labuan. Being first-time parents was like a culture shock to us. Marriage after kids requires great adjustments—no more date nights, no more eight hours of peaceful sleep, always in a hurry.

Despite all the difficulties, I think I appreciated our love so much more when we became parents. I felt like, if I was with the wrong person, this whole parenting journey would be so much harder. *Alhamdulillah.* It is in the way you see your spouse taking care of your child, the way you see them as a parent, that you will find the romance is still there, even deeper, and the love is just getting stronger.

Sadly, the role of a father is always underrated and underappreciated. When he changes his children's diapers, feeds them, plays with them; they said he is babysitting. When he cooks for the family, cleans the house, washes clothes; they said he is helping. But no, what he did was parenting. He was fathering. The failure to fully acknowledge a father's duty is perhaps the reason why fatherhood sometimes is being underappreciated in society while motherhood is over-glorified.

But the hadith taught us that no child can truly repay his father.

Abu Hurayrah reported:

The Messenger of Allah (peace be upon him) said, "No child can compensate his father unless he finds him as a slave, buys him, and sets him free."

[Ṣaḥih Muslim]

57: To Love with Discipline

I have always been passionate about teaching. I was fortunate enough to be allowed to teach three batches of university students in the Philippines. But after marriage, I needed to resign as I have to follow my husband to our new home in Malaysia.

After getting married and becoming a full-time housewife, I was stricken with extreme boredom. One random day, an idea suddenly came out of the blue where I thought, why not offer a free Qur'anic class to the neighbourhood? So, I discussed with my husband and took the courage to send a message in our residence's WhatsApp group, announcing that I will be offering Qur'anic back-to-basic class for free. *Alhamdulillah*, it seems that the *rizq* of teaching runs in my blood.

I recalled there were three to five interested neighbours. One of them was a seven-month pregnant woman, with three small children. I remember during our first class which she struggled to attend because her two-year-old daughter was tagging along.

During our second class, I made an appointment to have the class at the comfort of her home as I realised there was no better way to teach the Qur'an than to focus on the student individually. She had to put her daughter to sleep in the bedroom before she can come forward to me in the living room and start our lesson.

Her eagerness in learning the Qur'an despite her status of being a mother of four truly humbled me. I was even impressed when I heard how she would enforce her sons to pray at the masjid every day, although she understands how tired her children are from school. I as a wife, sometimes feel guilty to wake my husband up before *fajr* to pray at the masjid knowing how tired he was from work. I wonder what more a mother's guilt towards her children. Let us train our hearts, to love with the discipline.

> "O' you who have believed, let not your wealth and your children divert you from the remembrance of Allah."
>
> [al-Munafiqun, 63:9]

She also has something in common with me. Our husbands work in the oil and gas industry, go offshore for months and come home for only days before leaving again. She has to handle everything on her own in the absence of her husband. To me, her commitment in dedicating her motherhood to Allah, truly stand as an inspiration.

She taught us that:

1. **Never give up on seeking knowledge.** Even though you may not have the means, as long as you have the intention, then that is a good start already. This student of mine already has the intention to study the Qur'an for so long but she does not seem to know how or when until I moved to the same residency and we met. Nothing is impossible, with such a noble intention, Allah will surely show us the way.

2. **Who you are in the past do not define who your children will be, as long as you are committed to change.** The power to change is in your dedication.

3. **Love but never spoil.** Saying this, let us re-evaluate how we deal with our children. Allah says in the Qur'an,

   "And know that your properties and your children are but a trial that Allah has with Him a great reward."

   [al-Anfal, 8:28]

CHAPTER 5: LESSONS LEARNED IN LIFE

"*If a person has the ability to reflect, he will find lessons in everything.*"

[Sufyan ibn Uyaynah]

58: Listen to Your Self-Talk

Throughout my life, I noticed there were times when Allah has made my intentions a reality although I have not properly asked for them yet in my prayers. Just like this one time, when I wish I could find ways to continue pursuing my Qur'an journey with a certified teacher despite being a full-time direct breastfeeding plus working mother. I came up with the thought when I was in the shower.

The next two days, surprisingly I found myself successfully enrolled in an academy. But yes, I had to do research on the academy, submit my application, call the person in charge, attend interviews and many more because nothing comes easy.

Looking back, it is dreamlike how things just happened so fast with one random thought in the shower!

This reminds me of Imam Abu Hanifah. When he was on his deathbed, he started to make numerous intentions of doing great things like building a madrasah. His students asked him why he did so when he knew he did not have long to live. The imam replied, "If I were to die, then Allah would give me the rewards for my intentions. If I were to live, then Allah would make these intentions a reality."

Therefore, in your moment of silence, do listen to your random thoughts. It could be a *hidayah* from Allah, giving us the idea of how to be better. Now it is upon us, to have the courage to pursue that thought. May Allah grant us the *taufiq* (divine help).

59: Now or Never

Over the years I learned that there is no truly a stage of life considered as "not that busy". When I was a student, I thought I would have more time after I have finished with all the studies and exams. But after completing my education, my life was busy with work. Then, my life was busy with getting married and adjusting to life with a new status.

Now that I am a mother, I think I am busy because I have an infant requiring full attention. But to think of it, I have only two children while my friend has three and yet she is very productive.

As they said, no one is too busy in this life. It is all about priority. I guess the solution is to change our mindset. So, if you are planning on taking a Master's Degree, or memorising the Qur'an, or reading a list of books, then you have to make an effort to look for the time in pursuing these goals. Now or never!

Sharing below the five habits of highly successful Muslims extracted from *The Daily Reminder.* Stay inspired, say no to procrastination, and keep up the good faith!

1. **Wake up early**

   The earlier you start your day, the more things you will be able to accomplish.

2. **Read a lot**

   The best investment for yourself is to gain more and more knowledge. Read self-improvement books, the story of the prophets, and the best of all is Qur'anic studies.

3. **Make your mental health a priority**

   Mental health is important as physical! Stay positive, follow inspirational speakers, and listen to beneficial lectures. Stop befriending negative and judgemental people.

4. **Do not get distracted with people's journey**

   Be inspired by others but never compare yourself to them.

5. **Your time is finite and limited**

   Every day, ask yourself what improvement have you done for yourself today. Improve and refine, improve and refine, and improve and refine!

اللَّهُـمَّ إِنِّي أَعُوذُ بِكَ مِنْ الْهَمِّ وَالْحُزْنِ
وَالْعَجْزِ وَالْكَسَـلِ وَالْبُخْلِ وَالْجُبْنِ وَضَلَعِ
الدَّيْنِ وَغَلَبَةِ الرِّجَالِ

'O' Allah, I take refuge in You from anxiety
and sorrow, weakness and laziness, miserliness
and cowardice, the burden of debts and from
being overpowered by men.'

[Sunan Abi Dawud]

60: Make a Flower Bloom

I am quite a melodious reciter of the Qur'an. My *ustadha* commented that due to my melody, I have compromised the consistency of elongation in *'mad'* rulings. She then asked me to imagine a cake with a beautiful icing layer. The melody of the Qur'an is just like the icing, it aims only to beautify the cake but it must not compromise the taste of the cake because it is better to have a beautiful and delicious cake, and not a beautiful cake that is not delicious.

I love the way she rectified my error. Soft and gentle, I did not feel humiliated, in fact, I felt encouraged, making me strive harder. It made me self-reflect. Sometimes due to my excessive zealous in encouraging others to do good, I tend to be harsh and judgmental without realising it. This is a constant battle for me. Instead of inspiring, I condemn. Perhaps my method of rectifying the error can be a greater error than the error itself.

It reminds me of how the Prophet (peace be upon him) used to deal with people using techniques that would instil in them the eagerness to do good; he made them feel that they were close to good, even if they had erred. Once, there was a man seeking to pledge alliance to Prophet (peace be upon him) but he left his parents crying. The Prophet (peace be upon him) was neither harsh towards him, nor did he belittle his action, nor demean his intelligence. The man had come with good intentions and thought that what he was doing was best. So the Prophet (peace be upon him) simply said, "Go back to them and make them laugh." [Sunan Abi Dawud].

That was it. The Prophet (peace be upon him) looked at his goodness and surpassed his evilness.

So you see, choosing the right words is a skill not given to many. A wise man will seek softness in speech, despite the bitterness of truth. In being honest, he prioritises *adab* (manners). In doing *da'wah*, he intends to invite not to 'kidnap'. Just like continuous rain that can soften a hard stone, it is also through rain, not thunder, that a flower blooms. When a flower does not bloom, we fix the environment it grows and not the flower itself.

The next time we want to remind others of their error, may we always remember that we deal with hearts and not bodies. Apply firmness only when necessary.

"Allah is gentle, and He loves gentleness. He rewards for gentleness what is not granted for harshness, and He does not reward anything else like He rewards gentleness."

[Ṣaḥih Muslim]

61: The Abused Kindness

During my teenage to college years, I was very passionate about volunteerism. I believe that as a youth, despite not having a stable job yet and still studying, we can still help to make a difference in the world by contributing our time and energy to the *ummah* as volunteering for the sake of Allah may entail both bigger rewards which come when you are really in need in *dunya* and *akhirah*. Many times, we are surprised by the turns of an event that we never have expected.

In the story of Umm Mihjan, a poor, black-skinned woman who had no place to stay, so she lived in the Masjid of Al-Madinah and she used to clean the masjid and look after its upkeep.

Abu Hurayrah reported,

"A black woman used to clean the mosque. The Messenger of Allah (peace be upon him) missed her and asked about her. He was told that she had died. He (peace be upon him) said, "Why did you not inform me?"" (It seemed as if) they (Companions) considered the matter insignificant. Then he (peace be upon him) said, "Show me her grave."" When it was shown to him, he offered *janazah* (funeral) prayer over it and said, "These graves cover those in them with darkness, and Allah illumines them for the inmates as a result of my supplication for them."

(Ṣaḥiḥ al-Bukhari and Muslim)

Imam As-Suyuti commented that when you do something for the sake of Allah, you will receive the rewards and taste its pleasantness not only in the Hereafter but also in this life. This black woman who served her community by cleaning the masjid was honoured by the Prophet of mercy; he visited her grave to pray for Allah's mercy and forgiveness for her.

Allah says in the Qur'an,

"Is the reward for good [anything] but good?"

(ar-Raḥman, 55:60)

When you sow the seeds of goodness, you will reap goodness. But sometimes in the journey of sowing goodness, challenges might come your way.

Once, I volunteered to teach Iqra' class to the children in our neighbourhood for free at my house. Somehow, I noticed, some of the parents left their children with me beyond what was agreed. They came to pick their children up only when the day has darkened. My intention which was supposed to be purely for teaching was polluted, as I felt like I was forced to babysit. I was frustrated.

In volunteering work, we sometimes work extremely hard and only Allah knows how much we have put our hearts into it. We dedicate our sacrifices, not in the pursuit of money or fame. But what people tend to forget is, a kind heart can endure when being ignored and taken for granted, but it may expire upon being abused.

To volunteers who face challenges like this, it is OK to feel frustrated. You are a human. You are not over-reacting. You are not overly sensitive. If it hurts you, it hurts you. In a moment like this, dare to say no without feeling guilty. Setting reasonable boundaries is healthy. Learn to respect, defend, and take care of yourself. We are afraid that there will be no more sincerity in our hearts when the sense of being forced is already present.

In doing good, there will always be challenges. Whenever you feel tired and want to give up, remind yourself that Allah sees our effort and He will provide. He will give credit when the credit is due.

"And whoever volunteers good—then indeed, Allah is Appreciative and Knowing."

[al-Baqarah, 2:158]

62: The *Barakah* of Time

After completing high school, I was accepted into one of the most prestigious boarding colleges where the students were among the best of the best in the country. It was a dream that came true for me to be able to study there, thus I promised myself that I would study hard and be the best I could be. So, I arranged my life schedule perfectly—having a good routine of classes from Monday to Friday, hanging out with friends on Saturday and going for a jog every morning on Sunday. Not to mention, my friends always invite us to pray at the mosque every Maghrib prayer and stay until Isha for short Islamic lectures. For months, I thought I was living the life of the best student—healthy mentally, socially, spiritually and physically. I believed that I have used my time wisely, as a student and as a Muslimah.

However, when the result of the first semester was released, my grade was not what I had expected. It was so disappointing.

As I was looking for an answer, I realised there was something I hid deep inside. I always felt that it was a waste of time to attend Islamic lectures or participate in any MSA (Muslim Student's Association) activity. I kept counting the time that I would spend if I were to join an Islamic lecture, versus staying in my room to study academic subjects. I questioned what benefits would I get if I was to attend madrasah, as compared to the benefits of reviewing my academic subjects and earning good grades. So, I turned down most invitations and focused on my studies.

This was my mistake.

Focusing on your studies is good. The not-so-good part is when you think any religious activity (e.g., listening to an Islamic lecture, attending madrasah classes, and reciting the Qur'an) will distract you from your studies and the causes of making you *a lesser achiever*. It shows that we are being selfish with the time Allah has gifted us.

One night during the Holy Month of Ramadan, we just came back from town and decided to perform our Maghrib and Isha' at the small praying room in our dormitory block before heading to the big mosque for the *tarawih*. There were two Muslimat who came into the room and called our attention.

"Can you all please stay for a little while before we go to the mosque? Just want to have small *usrah* (circle) among us", said one of them. In my heart (as stingy as I usually am), I thought it was another waste of time as I wanted to go back early and study. She started by reciting surah al-Baqarah, verse 261.

"The example of those who spend their wealth in the way of Allah is like a seed [of grain] which grows seven spikes; in each spike is a hundred grains. And Allah multiplies [His reward] for whom He wills. And Allah is all-Encompassing and Knowing."

[al-Baqarah, 2: 261]

She then added, "Out of thousands of students in this college, have you ever wondered why you were among the chosen ones to be here (in this small *usrah*) right now? Allah loves you. Some students studied all night long but did not absorb any knowledge. On the other hand, some students studied for five minutes, but they grasp everything. See? If you spend some time for Allah—reciting the Qur'an, visiting the mosque, performing *tarawih*, attending Islamic lectures; you will be surprised that you could do more in twenty-four hours than you think! *In sha Allah*. This is because according to the Qur'an, Allah gives multiple folds to those who spend in the way of Allah.

Allahuakbar! Upon hearing that from them, I felt like I was slapped. Indeed, I realised how I have wrongly used Allah's gift of time for me. How dare I am, to think that spending time for Allah will only take away my time for *dunya*.

If there is one thing that I can advise to the students, then it would be to spend time for Allah and never ever think that doing something for Allah will only distract you from your academic goals. Rather, it is by doing something for Allah that He will grant you both *dunya* and *akhirat*.

One of the *salaf* (righteous predecessors) said:

"Whenever my portion of reciting the Qur'an would increase, the *barakah* (blessings) in my time would increase. And I would not cease increasing in reciting until the amount of my recitation reached ten *juz*".

[Thail Tabaqat-il-Ḥanabilah]

Strive for the *barakah* of time! Whether you are a student or working, do not be afraid to spend time for Allah. After all, we are just borrowing Allah's time, aren't we?

63: Retention is by Repetition

All this time I thought the greatest challenge of being a reviewer is to finish as many books as you can in so little time. I was wrong. Anyone can finish a book cover to cover in one day if they have the desire. The problem is not how much you know, but how much you remember. How depressing it is that you need to go back to chapter one all over again, not once, twice or thrice, every time you forget.

Now I understand why the great scholars said in seeking knowledge, one must be patient. No mental pressure can ever beat this kind of emotional stress. It is exactly the time like this that you just want to give up. But how can we give up, when the only cure we know is:

RETENTION IS BY REPETITION.

Constant repetition is a long-term consistency, and long-term consistency always beats short term intensity. It is what transforms average into excellence. So let the seekers of knowledge persevere in patience and constancy.

"O' you who have believed, persevered, and endured and remain stationed and fear Allah that you may be successful."

[Ali 'Imran 3:200]

May Allah grant us great patience in seeking knowledge, and may all this hard work, effort and knowledge benefit this *ummah* in the future.

64: Great Things Take Time

When I was in university, I was worried sick of failing my subjects and repeating semesters but thankfully I passed all of them and graduated successfully, *Alhamdulillah*. After graduation, I was worried sick for not being able to pass my professional exam but the result turned out to be the best when we expected the worst, *Alhamdulillah*. After the board exam, I was worried sick even more because apparently, the real world does not judge you according to your grades, even though you were torn apart between upholding your belief or desperately selling your principle to get such a grade and survive in this cruel world. But by the Mercy of Allah, I was hired a few months later, *Alhamdulillah*.

These were what happened to me two years after graduation. So, I say to the fresh graduates, relax! You will graduate, you will get a job, you will become an adult, you will find someone who loves you.

Great things take time!

The Qur'an tells us that Allah created the universe in six days even though He could have made them in a split second; why? Qurtubi said that from amongst the Divine Wisdoms, one of them was to teach us the importance of diligence and deliberation. Good things take time to build and prepare.

Transforming yourself into something great needs an investment of time and energy. So, persevere, but enjoy yourself in the process of transformation.

Yours sincerely,

Aiyen Segovia

Batch 2014 Graduate.

65: Garden of Paradise

Deep inside, I am always inspired to see a whole family attending an Islamic lecture or class. A father, despite being busy at work; and for a mother, despite the chaos in handling her children and the household; they can still find time to bring their whole family in the gathering of knowledge seekers. They are the epitome of *family goals to Jannah* as in the Qur'an,

> "Gardens of perpetual residence; they will enter them with whoever were righteous among their fathers, their spouses and their descendants. And the angels will enter upon them from every gate, (saying), "Peace be upon you for what you patiently endured. And excellent is the final home."

> [ar-Ra'd, 13:23-24]

Everything that we want to last, be it a house or a car or even a relationship, requires regular maintenance. One of the many ways to improve and increase love between family members is by always bringing them closer to the remembrance of Allah.

"When a group of people assemble for the remembrance of Allah, the angels surround them with their wings, Allah's mercy envelops them, *sakinah* (tranquillity) descends upon them and Allah makes a mention of them before those who are near Him."

[Ṣaḥiḥ Muslim].

It is only when we became parents ourselves that we realised how kind and considerate it is that organisers of any Islamic symposium/class, prepare a special room for parents with toddlers. They provide an environment for us which shows that children are very much welcomed too. Their support makes you aware that indeed, having little children should never be a hindrance in the path of seeking knowledge. It is the spirit like this, which encourages a whole family to keep attending Islamic classes.

As a mother, I must compliment the effort of these organisers who provide a 'mother-kids' corner' so the mothers can listen attentively to the lectures while their children can safely play in that space without disturbing others. In the spirit of building a family of *sakinah mawaddah warahmah* in this *ummah*, I hope to see more mother-children friendly zone in these gardens of Paradise. I pray that more family will spend their family weekend by attending a weekend Islamic lecture, or simply bonding by watching many beneficial Islamic videos together at home.

May we be united in *Jannah* together with our loved ones.

"Enter Paradise, you and your kinds, delighted."

[az-Zukhruf, 43:70]

66: A Teacher for Life

I always have deep respect for teachers. I believe they played an important part in determining who we are today. I remembered a teacher way back in my high school who is indeed one of a kind. It was through her (may Allah grant her goodness), that Allah has guided me to wear hijab.

1. **She used to call us by our FULL name.**

    I really salute this teacher as a long name is not an excuse for her not to call her students by their full name. She says every one of us is given a beautiful and meaningful name by our parents. We should honour it. She believes that simply calling the person's meaningful full name instead of their nicknames, is already a repetitive *du'a'* to the name bearer.

2. **She NEVER came in late to class.**

    She is very meticulous with the money she earns. She makes sure that she deserved every cent of it. If she will be paid RM60 for sixty minutes, she will make sure that she worked sixty minutes to earn RM60. This is one of the attitudes that I respect much about her and leave such a great impact on me especially when I entered the working world. This principle should be applied to all jobs, where we give our salary every justice it should get. She taught me that, as Muslims, we must seek a blessed income. Indeed, a believer should fear Allah and not his boss.

Ibn Qudamah (Allah has mercy on him) said,

"Thus were the women among the Salaf, when a man would leave his home, his wife would say to him: "Beware of haram earnings. For we can be patient upon hunger, but we cannot be patient upon the Hellfire."

[Mukhtasar al-Minhaj]

3. *She inspired me to wear HIJAB.*

The biggest gift she gave me—MY HIJAB. It is true, that everything comes from Allah (Glorified and Exalted is He) and I am thankful that it is through this teacher of mine, I have made a *hijrah* (transformation) to myself in wearing proper hijab. Once, she requested me to make a poster for a campaign about *'aurat*. I did not understand why she gave me that task, I just completed it for the sake of grades. I have made that poster with all my heart and made it beautiful. When my *ustadha* posted it on the bulletin board in the hallway in school, I found something is missing. How can I ask people to wear hijab if I myself did not wear it properly? Can I guide people to cover their *'aurat* when they know the one who made that poster is not doing what she said?

"O' you who have believed, why do you say what you do not do? Great is hatred in the sight of Allah that you say what you do not do."

[as-Ṣaf, 61:2-3]

Astaghfirullah! That moment, a realisation hit me hard and I wished to change. May Allah grant her rewards for her unique way of *da'wah. Ameen.*

We have countless teachers who teach science, mathematics and other subjects. But for a teacher who teaches life values and changes you to the core of your individuality, is rare among the rarest. I am blessed to find such a teacher, for what truly remains in a person's life in the future is not intelligence, rather a moral attitude eventually.

Like me, there will be such a time when I am no longer a working woman. But I will always stay as a daughter, a wife, and a mother to my family. By that time, I may need science to raise my children, but more than that, I need values that should be uprooted in their upbringing. So, I would like to take this opportunity to say thank you to all my teachers. I am what I am today because of all of you.

67: A Journey of Teaching Children

I was fortunate enough to be given the opportunity of offering free Qur'anic classes to the children in my neighbourhood. The youngest students in my Qur'an class were Elfateh and Ainul, who were around five to six years old. They were just learning *alif ba ta*. The greatest challenge in teaching kids is, they have a shorter span of attention compared to adults thus it takes greater patience to handle them.

Unlike adults who attend Qur'anic classes because they are aware of the great rewards behind it, children, on the other hand, are mostly forced by their parents and they do not know why they have to learn the Qur'an. It is important that a teacher would try his or her best to create a lovely learning environment for them. Hence, first thing first, make them happy with the class so they will keep looking forward to attending.

Sharing below are some tips that might be useful to those who wish to teach children. May this benefit.

1. FOOD OFFERINGS

Giving food to them is by far the most effective one although it is the most criticised one. I noticed their attention span lasted for fifteen minutes only, then their eyes started to wander around the house. I need to give them a break, but I promised them if they can answer me correctly, they will have food as a reward. Of course, you need to ask permission from their parents in case there are allergies or house rules on forbidden food.

Some people might disagree, but what I like about offering food is aside from giving *ṣadaqah*, it is also your opportunity to teach them *sunnah* of eating and drinking. Teach them to say *Bismillah* before eating and use the right hand always.

I remember Elfateh, there was once when he intentionally said *Bismillah* out loud before drinking just to make sure I know he does what I taught. Such a sweet boy, *Allahumma bariklahu*.

2. LIMITATION

Limit your lessons and time of teaching per day. Teaching two to three *huruf* (alphabets) for thirty minutes every day is enough. I usually teach them new lessons first, before reviewing past lessons because they have one hundred percent attention during the beginning of the class as compared to later.

3. ACTIVITIES

Children love activities. I use drawing techniques so they will not get boring, and exercises help to improve their memory. My husband donated a small whiteboard, so the students can write then erase it anytime. At the end of every exercise, I will rate them and give them five stars if they performed excellently. Kids can easily be lured with five stars and they will work so hard for it.

4. LEARNING IN A GROUP

Unlike adults, teaching children is best if they are in a group. I only have two students at the moment, so I can fully supervise them. A healthy competitive environment will encourage them to try harder.

5. STORY-TEACHING TECHNIQUE

I use a story-description style to introduce new *ḥarf* like "a smile with two eyes" for ت, "a fat snake with one eye" for خ, "two small smileys with one big smile" for س. And I made up a lot of stories for each *ḥarf*. I am not sure if it works, but so far it helps them to remember.

Teaching children, be it ABC or 123 what more *alif ba ta,* is a long-term investment to *akhirah.* Be inspired to teach one; your little sister. Your son. Your neighbour's kid. Even just once in our lifetime, put it on your wish list to invest in something like this. *In sha Allah.*

The Prophet (peace be upon him) said,

"The best among you (Muslims) are those who learn the Qur'an and teach it."

(Ṣaḥiḥ al-Bukhari)

Disclaimer: All tips are based on personal experiences.

68: The Gift That Keeps Giving

Once in a mall, I saw various offers of the latest smartphones plus an internet package with payments as low as RM200 per month for a contract of two years.

Did you know, in the Philippines, with less than RM200 every month for at least one year, you can already sponsor a needy student in a madrasah? By the end of the contract, you will have a Qur'an memoriser who shall spread his knowledge to the next generation. Compare this if you commit to buy the phone, where perhaps you will fall in love with another brand-new phone again by the time your contract has ended.

I remember my husband's advice; a wise man will buy an old house rather than a new car because he sees the profit of property investment. Likewise, in looking for potential charity, try to work on a legacy that will benefit you not only in this world but also in the Hereafter eternally.

I believe that the best gift to exchange with someone is the Noble Qur'an. Imagine if you have RM1 and your friend have RM1 and you both exchanged, both of you will still have RM1 each at the end. But when you exchange the gift of the Qur'an to each other, at the end of the day you both will have two rewards each—your recitation and his recitation using your gift. This is indeed a very profitable kind of exchange system. Be inspired to have that 'exchange the Qur'an gift' with your best friends.

Prophet Muhammad (peace be upon him) said,

"Exchange gifts, as that will lead to increasing your love for one another."

[Ṣaḥīḥ al-Bukhari]

Among other gifts that keep giving even years after you passed away:

1. **Teach someone beneficial knowledge who will highly apply them for the rest of their lives**

    Tips: Look for at least one potential kid whom you can be the first to teach him ABC or Arabic letters or numbers.

2. **Give copies of the Noble Qur'an to your friends who love to recite the Qur'an**

    Tips: My best friend gifted me a Qur'an before. The Qur'an is a common one but she decorated the cover beautifully using her creativity, even attached a cute bookmark with related inspiring hadith. You can try this! Make a unique one and give it to your beloved friend.

3. Give away beneficial Islamic books (recommendation: *Don't Be Sad, Enjoy Your Life, Rekindle Your Life*)

These books are great influences that can transform readers, especially with regards to Islamic mannerism.

Plant a tree. Donate to build a mosque. Share online beneficial *du'a'*. Participate in the *da'wah* cause and many more.

The Prophet Muhammad (peace be upon him) said:

"He who called people to righteousness, there would be a reward for him like the rewards of those who adhered to it, without their rewards being diminished in any respect."

[Ṣaḥiḥ Muslim]

69: Back In 2012

When I was still admitted to the hospital after giving birth to my second born, my husband at home sent me some graduation pictures of him from Northern Arizona University back in 2012. It got me thinking that in 2012, I was still in my third-year university and still figuring out my life.

There were times when I wondered about the future like "What will I be ten years from now?" and "What is my future husband doing right now?"

Today, answering my 2012 self-thoughts, apparently in 2012 my future husband was just graduating and we were total strangers separated by continents. Today, here I am, migrated to KL with two babies. Today, my career is not even related at all to what I have learned back in university!

As humans, we tend to anticipate what will happen next but we also yearn for the ability to go back and change the past. But there is beauty in accepting your *Qadr*.

Imam Aḥmad Ibn Hanbal said,

"If al-Qadr (destinies, decrees, paths of life) were presented to man, he would choose the one that Allah has already chosen for him."

Only a few years down the line would you understand why things happened the way they did. You will realise everything that happened to you was nothing but a blessing from Allah.

So, let life happen! Believe that someone somewhere is made for you forever, and if that certain opportunity is written for you, it will surely be yours eventually. Have hope that one day, you will be staring at all the blessings you used to always dream about.

70: Behind the Bars

When I was still working with the Department of Health as a medical lab scientist, my task was to visit the different health centres in rural areas to conduct HIV/AIDS testing. One day, we were assigned to visit the city jail to test some of the inmates for the said disease. It was my first time to visit such a place and I was informed that the place was filled with almost three thousand prisoners altogether.

When we were there, the male staff nurse-in-charge told us that these people rarely have visitors like us, but there is this one doctor who would voluntarily do free medical check-ups every Sunday and even provide them with free medicines.

It was just so sad to know that, apparently there were one hundred of them in a cell! Can you imagine? They were so congested in one room. All of these prisoners were still on trial and were charged with various crimes including drugs, rape, murders, terrorism, and many more.

Some people died in this prison and when no family member came forward to claim their dead bodies, the government would just bury them in a mass grave. What could be sadder than living as a lifetime prisoner and dying as an outcast?

When I look at the faces of these prisoners, they looked like us—so innocent. That is why they said, looks can be so deceiving. Hence the saying, "never judge a book by its cover".

Alḥamdulillah, dealing with HIV testing has exposed me to the dark side world of prostitution and the opportunity to see the reality of living behind the bars.

It reminds me that, every one of us is fighting a battle that only Allah knows. But whatever life has taken you to, just remember that Allah's mercy is greater than our sins. Never lose hope in Allah. He gives the hardest battle to the strongest soldiers only. Allah is The Most Forgiving, Most Merciful.

"Every son of Adam is a sinner, but the best of sinners are those who repent."

[Jami' at-Tirmidhi]

71: Taiwan Takeaways

One of my *dunya* goals is to bring my mom on a trip abroad as she deserves all the happiness in the world. It was in November when I had the privilege to bring my mother to visit a country that is not recognised as a country but contained many of Allah's miracles in it—Taiwan!

I must say, the best part of having your mum on a family vacation is instead of spending NT$100 for breakfast at the local restaurant, your mum can prepare you the best meal ever with only PHP100! We never thought that she would cook all of our favourite food from the Philippines and brought it to Taiwan, knowing these foods are hard to get in West Malaysia. A mother will always be a mother.

Whenever I visited a beautiful country, especially the ones with chilly cold weather like Taiwan, I wished I lived there and felt that the locals are blessed. But I realised in most of my journeys so far, as Muslims we will struggle here and there. Difficulties in finding halal food, prayer rooms, not to mention the high cost of living and overworking culture.

Perhaps my husband is right, that some countries are nice to visit but not to live in. The ability to express your faith freely and practise your rituals easily is a huge blessing.

We are still thankful for Malaysia despite the heat.

When we were in Taiwan, we visited Golden Waterfall. It is famous for its stones that are naturally gold in colour due to the acidic surrounding. We also got to witness the unique rocks at Yehliu Geopark, which can be found only in Taiwan. Just like what our tour guide loves to say, "These beautiful sceneries can only be seen in Taiwan. They are God's gifts from Heaven to Taiwan."

"In the Qur'an, Allah invites his servants to attain *ma'rifah* (knowledge) in two ways. The one, by contemplating the creation. The other, by meditating upon the Qur'an and contemplating its meanings. The first is His signs that are seen and witnessed. The second, His Signs that are read and understood."

[Ibn al-Qayyim]

It is awe-inspiring that there is always something special about His creation in all the different lands. May we attain *ma'rifah* through it.

Note for Muslim travellers:

☑ Make lots of *du'a'* because the *du'a'* of travellers are accepted.

☑ Never leave morning and evening *adhkar* for protection

☑ It is prescribed for one to leave the fixed *sunnah* prayers during travel, except *witr* and the *sunnah* of *fajr*. [Shaykh 'Abdul-Azeez Bin Baz]

"Travel through the land and observe how He began creation. Then Allah will produce the final creation. Indeed Allah, over all things, is competent."

[al-Ankabut, 29:20]

72: Venice—Little Wish Granted

The first time I laid my eyes on the images of Venice City, little Italy in the Philippines, on the internet, I was mesmerised by its picturesque scenery. I wanted to visit that place but never even once did I dare to say it out loud or even include it in my prayers because I thought, what kind of *du'a'* is that? There are so much bigger and more important matters to ask for from Allah, rather than just personal leisure.

But on June 5, 2016, I stepped foot in that stunning city and locked my eyes in its colourful structures. I was sent there by my company for a seminar. I was placed in one of the classiest hotels. I had my best friend who was living there temporarily for school, to tour me around. You see, the ticket was sponsored; the hotel was free, and I had the best tour guide ever. Everything was unexpected, everything was not even a plan.

As I reflect, I have learned that you can be realistic in everything but when it comes to prayer, please ask for the impossible. If Allah listens to your ridiculous wish that you whispered shyly deep down in your heart, how can He not listen to your desperate call that you have been asking for out loud in all your prayers?

"Call upon Me, I will respond to you."

[Ghafir, 40:60]

With the surprises from time to time, I am even more a grateful believer of *as-Sami'* (The All-Hearer).

73: Covid-19: Tomorrow is Not Promised

I was browsing through my photo album and saw a family vacation picture of ours that was taken in 2019 in Hong Kong, just fourteen days before their country's first protest in that year which then led to serious chaos of that nation. Just exactly fourteen months after that picture was taken, COVID-19 attacked the globe.

Perhaps there is beauty in romanticising the past. You are browsing at the old photos and realised that everything we have is all privileges. It is astonishing how things changed in just a blink of an eye. Peace was taken away in the span of fourteen days, and the world turned sick in just fourteen months.

But if it were not because of these sufferings, we would not know how the blessings of peace and health have been underappreciated and taken for granted. The freedom to go out of your house whenever you want, let alone the freedom to travel, was undervalued. It is making us all understand what we take for granted. If anything, this teaches us that tomorrow is not promised.

I hope at the end of this pandemic, may we never again take for granted a family reunion, happy wedding ceremonies, a Saturday night out, a crowded mall, or even a boring Monday routine because apparently, a regular normal pattern is a life in itself. May we come out better for each other because of the worst.

I pray that when this is finally over, we will be free to feel the world. But, will freedom ever feel the same again?

'Ali ibn Abi Talib (may Allah be pleased with him) said:

"Seize of what you have left of your life and do not keep saying, 'Tomorrow, and the day after tomorrow, for verily those before you were ruined because of their persist wishful thinking and their procrastination until suddenly, the command of God overtook them while they were heedless."

74: Covid-19: Absence of Fear

It was still week three of the Movement Control Order (MCO) in Malaysia due to the COVID-19 outbreak, but I had to bring my children to the clinic for their vaccination appointment. It was my first time to drive out after being home, quarantined for so long. It was scary going out amid a global pandemic, what more bringing these vulnerable little people, but a mother needed to do what a mother needed to do.

To think of it, how courageous are the parents and front-liners who have to go out every day because they have to. It is not that they are being fearless of the outbreak, but rather the judgment that something else is more important than fear. These people truly show us that courage is not the absence of fear, but a manifestation of love under pressure.

On the other hand, when "staying at home" has been imposed all over the world, it got me thinking—what about people who are homeless? What about victims of family abuse where the school is the only safe place? What about people who are stranded somewhere due to flight cancellation?

"Staying at home" is hard for front-liners, it is also hard for workers of daily wages. In this time of the global pandemic, you will realise nothing is more important than empathy for another human being's sufferings. We have to feel for one another if we are going to survive this pandemic with pride.

The Messenger of Allah, (peace be upon him) said,

"The parable of the believers in their affection, mercy, and compassion for each other is that of a body. When any limb aches, the whole body reacts with sleeplessness and fever."

[Ṣaḥih al-Bukhari and Muslim]

That being said, how privileged are so many of us that during a global pandemic, we can just stay at home reading, working, online studying, with a fridge full of food stocks. If we can afford hand sanitisers, clean water, soap, and face masks, then it is true when they say that the ways to ward off COVID-19 are accessible only to the affluent.

May we acknowledge this blessing upon us by complying with lockdown as the government imposed. Whether we are in a difficult or easy situation during this pandemic, it is not really about our state of affairs but more on our character during that state.

"Sulayman (AS) was rich and grateful, while Ayyub (AS) was afflicted and patient. But to both, it was said, 'An excellent servant. Indeed, he was oft-returning in repentance.'"

[Ṣad, 38:30 & 44]

Du 'a' for protection from diseases:

اللَّهُمَّ إِنِّي أَعُوذُ بِكَ مِنَ الْبَرَصِ، وَالْجُنُونِ، وَالْجُذَامِ، وَمِنْ سَيِّءِ الْأَسْقَامِ

"O' Allah, I seek refuge in You from leprosy, madness, elephantiasis, and evil diseases"

[Sunan Abi Dawud]

75: Covid-19: Choose to Spread Positivity

In these days of the COVID-19 pandemic where many have lost their jobs and the poor get poorer, I noticed how social media can be such a powerful tool in creating a philanthropic atmosphere. A simple charity post could invite many people to do a series of good deeds in the name of humanity. A picture of donation could influence others to follow. An upload intended for documentation to sponsor became an opportunity for other potential donors.

Ibn Hajr said :

"From the benefits of the plague and epidemic are: decreasing wishful hoping, perfecting good deeds, waking up from negligence, and preparing for the journey (to the next life)."

Nevertheless, it is quite disappointing that some people still manage to find criticism. Some volunteers were being accused of *riya'* (showing off). Perhaps the greatest charity we can do is to be kind to each other, do not judge, and give others the benefits of the doubt or remain quiet. Social media is also used to advertise negativity or non-beneficial activities. So, when there is an opportunity to encourage and lead the way in doing good, then let it be. There is a very thin line between bragging and inspiring.

To volunteers whose kindness was not only gone unappreciated but even abused, please know that people may destroy your image but they cannot take away your integrity and worthiness because no matter how they describe you, you will still be admired by those who know you better. Your presence has made a difference in their lives.

"And whoever volunteers good then indeed, Allah is Appreciative and Knowing."

[al-Baqarah, 2:158]

If you are aware of your intention, the glory is already yours. If you have a sincere purpose at heart for sharing and some misinterpret your message, it is not your business to try to convince them otherwise. That is their problem, not yours.

Be unapologetic in the pursuit of creating a better world.